The Holistic Homestead
How to Start an Interconnected Homestead

By Julia Hubler

The Holistic Homestead: How to Start an Interconnected Homestead
Copyright © 2017 Julia R. Hubler

"You shall not steal." —*Deuteronomy 5:19 (NKJV)*

ISBN: 154840506X
ISBN-13: 978-1548405069

All photos taken, and charts were taken, made or drawn by Julia Hubler. Except the picture of me—*taken by my sister. :)*
Soli Deo Gloria! *(Glory Be to God Alone!)*

This Book Is Dedicated...

To the Advancement of Christ's Kingdom

Here on earth as it is in heaven--*Soli Deo Gloria!*

"He shall have dominion also from sea to sea, and from the River to the ends of the earth...And blessed be His glorious name forever!

And let the whole earth be filled with His glory. Amen and Amen."

-Psalm 72:8 & 19 (NKJV)

Acknowledgements

I want to thank my family for all the support they've shown me through this whole book-writing process. Thanks dad for all of your encouragement! Thanks mom for helping me with editing and all of the tedious details that made this book possible!

Thanks Gaby, Emily and Maggie for all of your help, support and encouragement! I couldn't have done it without you all.

Thank you Mrs. Ronsick for your amazing friendship and editing job! I owe the organization of this book and so much more to you. Thanks!

Thank you Brooke and Christianna for all the fun times we've had talking about homesteading and everything! Thanks for your friendship, encouragement and editing help! *-Miss you Brooke! <3*

A big thanks to all my beta readers, for all your suggestions and support!

Thank you Aunt Debbie for your help with Photoshop and type design on the cover!

And last but not least, I want to thank Christ the King for everything He has done! *-Including His Sovereignty in making this book come to pass.*

To Him be all glory, honor and praise, both now and forever…

Amen!

Table of Contents...

...Table of Contents

------- Part 3: Indoor Homesteading -------

------ Part 4: Put the Pieces Together! --------

Introduction...

Homesteading is a **big** task! There are always things that keep you busy, and there's a lot to do. Before you know it, you're lost in the details of the "tree". You focus in on the nitty-gritty details, losing sight of the forest—your end goal. You end up forgetting the main purpose of your homestead.

The details are important! We'll go over lots of them as we proceed. However, without a clear over-arching goal or purpose, the homestead would be nothing more than a bunch of disjoined parts and pieces, strewn on the floor in utter chaos.

The Purpose of This Book...

This isn't a "how-to-do every little homesteading thing" book. It's more of a practical "how-to-think" or "how-to-use-the-'how-to'-books" book. I've included as many practical tips and pieces of advice I could think of that I've learned. I tried to stick to the tips and advice you *don't normally find* in other homesteading books.

It's easy to get so caught up in one 'how-to' project and lose sight of the big picture. This book brings together each item and shows you how they relate. Read those how-to books—you need them. Just view them through the lens of **holistic thinking!**

Holistic thinking is no more than an old way, coming back to life again. A holistic mindset takes *everything* into account. It views each piece in light of all the others with a consideration and concern for the **whole!**

Stop viewing everything in separate categories. Break down those hindering walls. See your homestead as an **intricate system.**

See how to turn your problems into your solutions. See how to think practically. See how to use what you have and save money. See where to start or where to refocus your vision and goals.

Throughout this book I'll show you many practical connections. Connections to help you see how *everything* in the homestead relates to the other pieces. I'll help you make the practical connections for your homestead. By the end, the goal is for you to see connections and know how to use the information and projects you find over the years. You should be able to see and know how they fit—or don't fit—on your homestead.

Most homesteading books are about how to have a mini "farm" in your backyard. This book takes the best of homesteading, Joel Salatin's methods, and permaculture and puts them all together, forming the holistic homestead.

What's in This Book?

I've included helpful and relevant quotes, pictures, charts, drawings, and how-to tips, etc. Tips you'll need when you're at home and you can't drive to the store. Tips to help you think outside the box.

The book is easy to use. It's pretty enough to give as a gift and yet practical enough to take outside. At the end there's a detailed index to help you find what you're looking for.

In the resources section, you'll find lots of resources for further reading and study. I can't possibly cover everything. I want you to have good information and reliable places to learn more. Personally, I always love to get a resource (book, DVD, etc.) which was recommended to me by a person I trust.

Bonus On my website, I have a webpage with all the resources I recommend in this book. It has links for all the resources listed, so it's quick and easy to find what you're looking for.

I also have all of the charts/drawings from the book in the Appendix. They're larger and all together for your convenience.

What This Book Is Not

- This book is not meant to be "the basic how-to homestead information book". There are many good books out there for that. In this book we're going beyond the basics. We're going to delve into the topics most homesteading books leave out. Topics that are important to a successful holistic homestead.
- This book is not meant to be a "dreaming about homesteading" book. It's designed to be helpful and practical—not full of fluff and nonsense. The pictures are meant to be helpful first and foremost. The charts are there to explain further the point I'm trying to convey.
- This book is not meant to be 100% new to you. One thing we'll do is make connections. While not every connection may be new to you, I hope many are. You may already be making connections, yet thinking of it it a different light can spark a new connection you hadn't thought of.

————————————

Raising and growing your own food is a huge job. Whenever you find yourself getting hung up over the details or you start to feel discouraged, **stop!** Zoom back out and look at the big picture. Look at the whole. See the beauty of the forest. Then zoom back in and take it one step at a time. God is faithful and He is in it all. "And we know that all things work together for good to those who love God..." —*Romans 8:28 (NKJV)*

I pray this book will show you much about homesteading and encourage you in your homesteading endeavors. May you advance Christ's Kingdom on the piece of earth He has entrusted to your dominion. To Him be all the praise!

Soli Deo Gloria! *(Glory Be to God Alone!)*

- *Julia*

"...and God said to them, 'Be fruitful and multiply; fill the earth and subdue it; have dominion over the fish of the sea, over the birds of the air, and over every living thing that moves on the earth.' ...Then God saw everything that He had made, and indeed it was very good."
—*Genesis 1:28 & 31 (NKJV)*

---> Part 1 <---

The Holistic Mindset

Chapter 1: Holistic, Permaculture & Homesteading...

Let's consider a few terms.

1. Holistic
2. Permaculture
3. Homesteading

These three terms together build a healthy homestead. The three go together hand in glove. They are essential if you want a holistic-permaculture-homestead. Consider the term homesteading as shorthand for the combination of holistic, permaculture, *and* homesteading.

1. Holistic—This means to take into account the whole of something. To see all the different parts (home, cow, chickens, goat, garden, etc.) and how they work together as a system.

On your homestead you're looking for examples to follow. You may not realize it, but you are. What does everyone see when it comes to farming, gardening, or raising animals? They usually see big monoculture farms.

Without even thinking we gravitate towards what we have seen. It's hard to realize how much this affects us. Think about it...we see crops in rows, and then we plant our vegetables in rows. Typical orchards are sprayed, and then we want to spray—when often times a flock of chickens would be *better* pest control.

We need to see the whole homestead and take every aspect into account. What if instead of planting your trees in perfect rows, you staggered them so there's less sunlight getting to the bottom and therefore fewer weeds? Plant things in between and around the trees. Plant a ground cover like clover to control the weeds. There are many options when you think about it.

Find connections and make the pieces fit together, while taking into account the whole of your homestead. *Think holistically.*

2. Permaculture—What is permaculture? Permaculture is very similar to a holistic mindset. Permaculture is the agricultural ecosystems that are designed to grow together so they are self-sufficient. This means you'll take multiple species and kinds (plants and animals) and let them grow together and benefit each other, for the sustainability of everything in the entire system.

You can learn much from permaculture. There's so much practical, in depth, how-to information in permaculture books, articles and videos.

One of the best things about permaculture is that it takes a *problem* and turns it into a *solution.*

Here are a few examples:
- "I have an ant problem" to "food for my guineas!"
- "I have rotting fruit on my orchard floor" is now "food for the chickens, ducks and/or geese!"
- "Mulberry trees are messy" versus "mulberry trees by the chicken coop provide the chickens with lots of dropped fruit and shade!"
- "I have weeds growing everywhere" becomes "dandelions make great goat feed!"

That's exactly what this book is about. Making connections and putting pieces together! It's a holistic way of thinking.

There's so much practical information to be learned from permaculture. Some of my favorite books for the homestead are technically permaculture books. *(See Resources Chapter, page 192.)*

3. Homesteading—Homesteading is working the land you own and growing food for your family. That's the *modern* version of it anyway.

Combine that with Permaculture and Holistic thinking, and you get...a holistic homestead. Since I've started telling people I was writing this book, I've had a few people ask me *what* homesteading is. I didn't even realize till they asked that many still think of homesteading as it was a few hundred years ago! Get a free piece of land and after working it a specified number of years—it's yours. That's not how it is anymore. Here's my definition of a modern, holistic homestead...

A Holistic Homestead:

A piece of land, however small or large, for which the owner takes into account all aspects of the natural and other resources.

He makes every piece work together in the most productive way, for the benefit of the entire system and everything therein.

Land, home, animals, plants and all things, down to the soil microbes—in essence every living thing—are brought under his dominion.

This will look different on every homestead. It will look different in varying climates, locations, and situations, and according to the homesteader's personal preferences. These differences are normal. The holistic mindset can be applied to all.

No more segmenting, fragmenting, or compartmentalizing every aspect of your homestead! Leave that in the dust.

Think of your homestead as a whole, and see it as an *intricate system.* Pursue a Holistic Homestead.

Chapter 2: Holistic Guidelines...

To help you see and think holistically, here are a few guidelines. There may be occasional exceptions, but as a general rule these apply to the holistic homestead.

There should be:
- Zero waste
- Connections, rather than isolation
- Something else should be benefitting. *How does it serve or help another part of your homestead?*

Why Isn't It Working?—If a part of your homestead isn't lining up with one of these, think, how can you make it connect? Here are a few questions to ask:

- Does our homestead need it, or would it be better off without it?
- Is my system wrong? Can I fix the problem with better or different management?
- Is the timing bad? Maybe it would be great for your homestead, but not at this moment under the present circumstances.
- Do I live in the wrong climate for it? In this case you'll want to abandon the prospect altogether.

Find the Problem, Then Make Things Work—Once you figure out what's wrong, go from there. It may be because of current circumstances, or it may never be right for your homestead. If it won't thrive in your climate, forget it and try something else. If your timing is wrong, wait till you're ready. Maybe you just need to slow down and take it one step at a time. You may think you should be able to do everything in the first few months of homesteading and bite off more than you can chew. Slow down a little and you'll get to it. Timing is important!

Optimizing what you have before moving to new territory is great. However, just don't wait too long or you'll never get anywhere. You'll always find new ways to improve and expand your homestead. That's a great thing! It would get boring if there was a time when you had nothing left to do. Don't get too caught up in perfection. Keep moving forward.

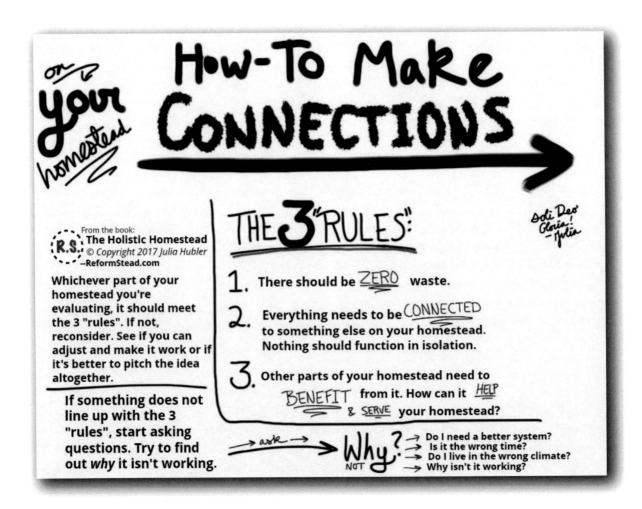

Everything Has a Job on the Homestead

Every critter on your farm needs a job. If something isn't working or producing, what purpose does it serve? Even beautiful flowers attract honey bees and other beneficial insects—*which is a job.*

If you don't see your cow or chickens as working you have one of two problems:
- They aren't working and you have a management issue.
- You don't **see** them as working.

The circumstances will vary based on your system and how you manage things. God created animals to work, and they do. The cow and sheep mow the grass. They spread fertilizer. Then the chickens spread it farther. The chickens tear down a compost pile. They also spread manure, etc., etc.

This is a big part of a holistically-minded homestead. Giving everything on your homestead a job is part of making the connections. Are you starting to picture a connected, holistic homestead?

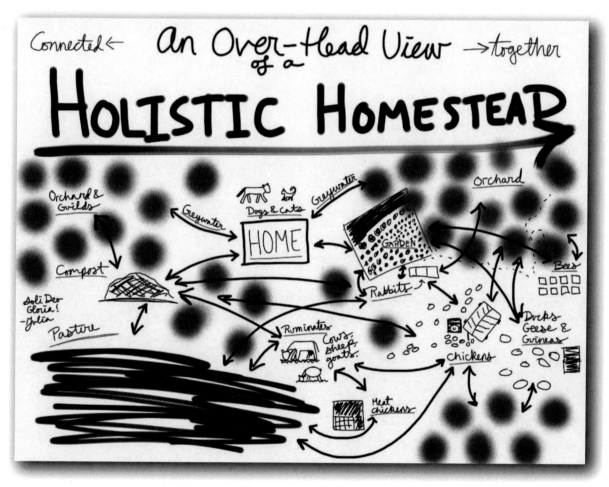

Working With Others

Team work on the homestead is *vital.* If you can't work well with other people now, you can learn. No single person can run and work an entire homestead.

When you work with others, each person is able to give the best of their skills to the project at hand. Not everyone does the same job equally well, so learn a job and "specialize" in it. You'll move on to the others. In the meantime, learn to be proficient at the task in front of you.

Work with multiple people and their different specialties. Then you can all work on one job and get it done with more speed and efficiency. Take butchering chickens for example. A few people can kill them, the next person is an expert plucker (especially with an electric pluckers you can use today *winking face*), then a few can work on gutting, etc. The job is done much more quickly this way than if every person butchered their own chicken. This applies to basically all homestead tasks.

Your family is a great starting place. Especially if you have a large family—think of all the different jobs in which the members of your family can specialize. Neighbors and friends broaden the list of jobs and specialties, and swapping skills is often a great option for homesteaders. (Depending on where you live, etc.)

Taking Steps

When you're learning about something new, often times it can seem overwhelming. There's so much to know and do. Don't get overwhelmed. Take it in steps.

Take organic food for example. When you first decide to go organic, often you can't afford to make a complete one-eighty in one day! So take it in steps. As you grow your own and start buying organic, it gets easier and you'll be able to do more as you go. It's a process.

Pick and choose what's most important to you, and do the best you can with what you have. Don't expect to get it all done overnight.

Chapter 3: Six Pivotal Points to Starting a Successful Homestead...

To homestead, you need both the mental and physical aspects of a homesteader. Here are three key aspects of each.

The Three Mental Aspects of Homesteading

Start homesteading with:
1. A willingness to fail
2. A love of learning
3. The right mindset

1. A Willingness to Fail— You need to be prepared to fail. After you fall down, don't stay there—get back up and do the best you can. Better to try and fail, than to not try at all.

Is it easier to remember to keep your head away from your goat's horns when she's in the milk stand before or after she nails you in the eye with them? *Ahem.* *Definitely easier after.*

It's interesting; we learn best and remember the most from our mistakes. It would be nice if we could learn more from reading and learning. I should have known to keep away from our goat's horns. I ***know*** now.

2. A Love of Learning—Get into this mindset now. It'll help a lot in the long run. When something breaks, figure out how *you* can fix it. However, there are things you won't be able to fix. If the septic goes out, or if you need a new well drilled, you'll probably have to hire someone. Thankfully, there are a lot more things you can do than you might think. You just need to be willing to fail and have a love of learning.

You can build your own chicken coop. Why pay someone else? It doesn't have to look 'professional' to work. Your chickens don't care what it looks like, as long as you keep the rain out. *Shhh, just don't tell them if the corner isn't perfectly square!*

Learn what you can, and do lots of projects on your homestead. Don't stress over everything. If you're a hard core perfectionistic, lay that down. Have fun! Get to the place where you see homesteading as more than chores. See homesteading as a way of life! You're learning something. That's valuable in and of itself.

Children Can Learn Too

There are many valuable skills to be learned on the homestead. Younger kids can get involved in the learning and work too. There are plenty of jobs to go around and even little children can learn to follow instructions and think for themselves. You can show them how and why you do what you're doing and encourage them to think. The homesteading life can be a great part of a healthy education.

---

3. The Right Mindset!—The other two could be wrapped up in the third answer...the right mindset. A *willingness to fail* and *love of learning* are both mindsets.

Everyone who starts homesteading begins with expectations. Some are legitimate, but many are often not. Starting your homestead with wrong notions is only going to lead to trouble and difficulties. You may, by God's grace, make it through and learn your lessons the hard way, but wouldn't you rather know what you're getting into first?

Your philosophy, views, opinions and concepts about life affect and shape your homestead way more than you realize.

What is your homesteading mindset *right now?* Is it normal to plant everything in straight rows, fertilize with whatever's "natural" at the nearest Home Depot, and after harvest throw the dead plants in the trash? What do you think when you see 1,201 dairy cows walking, sleeping and living in three feet of manure? What do you think when you see a huge field with corn and only corn growing? Is this normal?

If this seems normal to you, here's what your homestead will look like: you'll have one cow in a manure filled or clean pen. The chickens will be in their coop somewhere else. Don't forget the beautiful small-scale monoculture garden. *(Monoculture is growing acres of only one crop—corn, alfalfa, cotton, etc. This is the current conventional farming practice.)* Unless you've done some unconventional research, you'll plant the squash in one section, the corn in rows and the beans over there...etc. It's a homestead-scale monoculture farm.

Most Americans are immersed in a life of fragmentation. We want to put everything into their separate little boxes. We have politics over here, our faith over there, work life in this box, and family in still another box. This mindset causes problems which will flow over into how we homestead. *We hardly realize how much!*

When you bring that mindset to your homestead, you have chickens, a cow, goats, a dog, and a cat out back...and your family inside. You see few connections between them.

Your chickens are in their coop. You feed them their pelleted store-bought feed and collect their eggs every night. Meanwhile your cow is in a pen at the other end of the yard or even on pasture. Since they are separate, the chickens can't get over there and help her by eating the parasites, flies, or other bad bugs in her manure before they make your Jersey sick.

How about something as simple as feeding food scraps from your kitchen to the chickens? It may seem simple, but it's the small connections around your homestead that make a difference.

Approach homesteading with the notion that you'll be working with a bunch of disjointed pieces, and you will fail—yes, fail. Our culture predisposes you to see everything as disjointed and compartmentalized. That's a recipe for disaster on a homestead.

You need the right mindset! You need to make connections for your specific situation. Take your kitchen scraps to the chickens. Water an apple tree with greywater. Use your cow's (or any other animal's) manure as fertilizer on pasture, or make compost for the garden. While you're at it, find ways to do it with the least amount of *useless* work on your part. These are the kinds of connections you need to make on you homestead, and there are many more to come!

Ask God to show you connections, and then *see all the connections in His creation!* Look around. Open your eyes. Think and then think some more. *See* as many connections as you can. Look at what you have and *see* where you already have connections. *See* what others are doing and the connections they're making—*even if they don't see them.* Teach yourself to *see!*

It's basic but essential! The more pieces you put together correctly, the better and more beautiful the whole picture will be in the end.

Picture your homestead as a **puzzle.** Every single piece must fit. You know you have the right piece in place when it fits perfectly. If it's loose or you have to cram it in, the piece is in the wrong spot. Try something else. Keep trying until you fit the piece in the right spot. Then go on to the next piece.

It can be hard to teach yourself. You need to change the way you view things. When you see a cow in pasture with chickens running around her, what do you *see?* A pretty farm scene with a cow and chickens? Or do you see a cow eating grass with chickens spreading the manure. While they're at it, they're eating out the bad bugs and parasites which can make the cow sick.

When you begin to see things like this, you are making connections! You're *seeing* how the pieces fit together. Once you see the relationships, apply them to the rest your homestead.

Take a fresh look at your homestead. (Or picture your homestead-to-be.) Start by looking at the pieces you've already put together. Then look over your homestead—or homestead plans—and see where you *aren't* making the connections. Write them down, and find solutions.

I can't make all the connections for you. Your situation is going to have different pieces than mine. If you depend on someone else to see for you, you're missing the point, and you may miss important pieces. *You're* the person who needs to make the connections on your homestead. Teach yourself how to make the connections.

If you didn't start this way, that's fine. Readjust and learn to make connections with what you have. Homesteading has a learning curve. You improve as you go. It doesn't matter how far along you are. You can always make more connections—*as long as you have a holistic mindset.*

The Three Physical Aspects of Homesteading

Start homesteading:
1. With a good work ethic
2. Knowing you're always on duty
3. "You just do it!"[1]

1. A Good Work Ethic—Without lots of hard work, the homestead won't work. You need a good work ethic to make your homestead work. Homesteading is not a walk in the park. There's work to be done, and guess who's going to do it. The Bible uses ants as an example of a good work ethic.

"Go to the ant, you sluggard! Consider her ways and be wise,
Which, having no captain, overseer or ruler, provides her supplies in the summer, and gathers her food in the harvest." —*Proverbs 6:6-8 (NKJV)*

2. Always on Duty—Be ready to head on out and care for your homestead in rain, snow, or shine. You're on duty 24-7; 365 days a year.

Whatever's going on outside, you're in the middle of it. If the whole family's sick, someone still needs to go out and do chores. If one of your animals is sick, she may take a lot of tending and long hours through the night to get her better. When you take on homesteading, you're on call at any time.

3. "You Just Do It!"[2]—This is the key to success. This is how you get stuff done. This is where things happen. They get done in four simple words...

"A young fellow came to the farm for a few days to 'see how you get it all done.' When he got ready to leave, I asked what he discovered. He responded: 'I found out how you get it all done: **you just do it.**' How profound. He captured the essence of our success."
—From *You Can Farm,* by Joel Salatin[3] *[emphasis added]*

---> Part 2 <---

Outdoor Homesteading

Chapter 4: Grass Is Key!

Grow strong, healthy grass! It's one of the best things you can do for your homestead. There are so many benefits to healthy grass that it would be hard to overemphasize its importance.

The Benefits of Grass to Your Animals

A cow who lives in a feedlot never sees any grass. She's crammed in with hundreds of other cows living in unsanitary, putrefying fecal matter every day of her life. Diseases are easily transmitted in these conditions and she is fed the wrong food for her biology. Her life isn't as long as it should be. The poor conditions, wrong food and unnatural *everything* cause her to get mastitis, become lame, or get very sick. At which time she is sent to the butcher—years before a properly treated milking cow should be.

Compare her situation to a cow born in a grassy field. She has the sun, grass, and room to live they way she was *designed* to, from day one to the end of her life.

Which cow is going to be happier, healthier, stronger, live longer, need fewer vet visits, and give you better meat and/or milk?

The cow who's born and raised on pasture! Pastured animals (especially when rotationally grazing) have far fewer problems with parasites, worms, and other sickness causing "bugs" which wreak havoc in modern dairies and feedlots. They're eating the food their bodies were made to eat. Pastured animals are healthier. They need fewer— and hopefully no—antibiotics, vaccines, or vet visits. Healthy animals are also stronger and better able to fight off illnesses.

Chickens also are much healthier when raised on pasture. They love the grass, freedom and exercise! All the animals on your homestead will benefit from the pasture—not just the cows. They each will give and take different things.

The Benefits of *Multiple Species* on Pasture

A mixture of species is best for a few reasons. Cows, goats, sheep and poultry have different:

- Taste in grass and herbage
- Ways of eating grass
- Parasites and nutrients in manure

Tastes in Grass/Herbage—Different animals like different herbage. Goats like to eat a little of *everything*. Sheep and cows graze, and they like different types of grass and herbage. The different preferences they have mean more of your pasture will be eaten.

Different Ways Animals Eat Grass—When there are multiple species, all get to eat what they like best. They eat more of the grass in two ways: they eat the herbs and grasses they want and eat them at the height they desire. This improves your pasture because it's more efficient and there's less waste.

Cows and sheep eat the grass differently. Cows wrap their tongues around the blades of grass and yank it—then they chew it up. Sheep on the other hand, use the teeth in the front of their mouth to bite off the grass.

This means your cows wants to eat the long grass—and the sheep prefer the shorter grass—closer to the ground. A combination of cows, sheep and goats (especially for weeds), will be most efficient at utilizing your whole pasture.

More animals fit on your pasture than if you only had one species. If you can feed a cow on your pasture, add in a sheep and you'll get more out of it.

Parasites & Nutrients in Manure—Different animals have problems with different parasites. Diversity—combined with rotation (we'll get to that in a minute)—is key to natural parasite prevention.

"'Generally you have different parasites in different species (they are host-specific); they can't mature in the wrong host…You can break the life cycle of most parasites by multi-species grazing.' When equine-specific parasite eggs hatch, the larvae move onto grass plants where they might be ingested by a horse. If they're eaten by a cow or sheep rather than a horse, those larvae won't mature."
—*The Horse Your Guide To Equine Health Care (website)* [1]

This information is important, even if you don't have horses. It applies to your ruminants too.

In addition to parasite control, the pasture gets a wider variety of nutrients from their manure. *Healthy diversity always wins!*

"Cattle, goats, sheep, pigs, and poultry…have differing tastes in herbage and are host to different parasites, and their droppings contain different nutrients, too."
—*Keeping A Family Milk Cow* [2]

I found that quote amazing! It's a wonderful example of the stability of diversity.

Chickens also help keep the bad bug, fly, and parasite populations down. This means both your grass and animals are less likely to get sick or catch diseases. They also spread manure. This does two things: lets the manure absorb into the grass faster, and exposes the parasites and eggs so they dry up and die in the sun—unless the chickens eat them first.

"'…[chickens] are very good at spreading manure around—they tear up the piles to get any grain that wasn't fully digested or to eat the insects that live in fresh manure.' This also helps with parasite control; many of the parasite eggs passed in manure will be scattered—and dried out—and won't survive."
—*The Horse Your Guide To Equine Health Care (website)* [3]

Rotational Grazing Over Free Ranging

Going from feedlots to grass is a big improvement. Go from free ranging to rotational grazing, and you take another huge step in the right direction!

Free ranging is when you let the animals have access to all of your pasture, all at once. Rotational grazing is sectioning off small paddocks (either with electric fence, permanent fence, or movable fence panels) and rotating them through the smaller sections of pasture. These small areas can be tiny (a few hundred square feet each) or acres large, depending on the amount of land you have.

Rotational grazing ensures your whole pasture gets equal amounts of manure and grazing, with a break in between. It allows the land to rest and re-grow. It will then be ready for another batch of manure and grazing—on-and-on. *You get the full benefits the multiple species can give, when you rotationally graze.*

Let the animals roam around as they please and they'll have "favorite spots". You'll find them easily. There will be little to nothing growing there—and lots of fly attracting manure. All the while, the rest of your pasture will be stressed because it needs even grazing and manure—both of which you have in the wrong locations.

When you start rotationally grazing, you change your problem into a solution. The manure that's piled up in their favorite spot(s) now gets spread around as they graze your whole pasture more evenly.

I've read great testimonials where, after a few years of rotational grazing, the pasture is way better—thicker, longer and much greener. It's more productive than ever before. It's amazing what rotational grazing can do for a pasture!

The Amazing Benefits of Grass to Your Health

Healthier animals mean better food for your family. The meat, eggs and milk from animals who have been raised on grass have been shown to have fewer calories and more:

- Vitamin E
- Vitamin A
- Folic acid
- Omega-3 fatty acids
- CLA (a healthy fat)

> **CLA in Grass-Fed Livestock:**
> Looking a little more into CLA (or conjugated linoleic acid), we find it's a very important fat that can reduce your chances of getting cancer by over 50%. There is 3-5 times more of it in grass fed meats and even more than that in pasture-raised milk.

A cow, chicken, sheep, goat, etc., raised how it was designed to be raised = *A Healthier Meal.*

By having vitamins and nutritional co-factors, good fats through our eggs, meat and milk; we are fueling our bodies with what they need for better health. All this good stuff is what should be expected in any steak, fried egg, or glass of raw milk that has been raised on good pasture.

The Benefits of Grass to the Environment

Another bonus is how amazing grazing is for your land. By raising your livestock on grass you are being a good steward of the resources God has blessed you with. Pasturing uses less fossil fuels, enriches the soil with nutrients and natural fertilizers, and makes good use of manure. Instead of being a problem, manure is now your best ally to grow your soil microbes and grass. *A problem turned into a solution!*

It all boils down to this: God created cows to eat grass and run in the sunshine. He made the chickens to follow them and find the harmful bugs in their manure, eating them before they make the cows sick. ***Working with the way He designed His creation is always the way to succeed.***

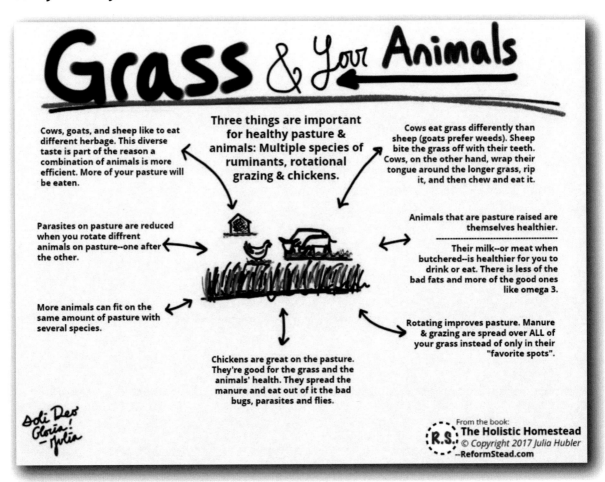

Grass & Your Animals

Cows, goats, and sheep like to eat different herbage. This diverse taste is part of the reason a combination of animals is more efficient. More of your pasture will be eaten.

Three things are important for healthy pasture & animals: Multiple species of ruminants, rotational grazing & chickens.

Cows eat grass differently than sheep (goats prefer weeds). Sheep bite the grass off with their teeth. Cows, on the other hand, wrap their tongue around the longer grass, rip it, and then chew and eat it.

Parasites on pasture are reduced when you rotate diffrent animals on pasture--one after the other.

Animals that are pasture raised are themselves healthier.

Their milk--or meat when butchered--is healthier for you to drink or eat. There is less of the bad fats and more of the good ones like omega 3.

More animals can fit on the same amount of pasture with several species.

Rotating improves pasture. Manure & grazing are spread over ALL of your grass instead of only in their "favorite spots".

Chickens are great on the pasture. They're good for the grass and the animals' health. They spread the manure and eat out of it the bad bugs, parasites and flies.

Soli Deo Gloria! --Julia

From the book:
R.S. **The Holistic Homestead**
© Copyright 2017 Julia Hubler
--ReformStead.com

Chapter 5: The Microbial Conscious Gardener...

I haven't counted, but I'm pretty sure there are one-thousand and one gardening methods online. *No one has trouble with their garden for lack of methods.*

It's overwhelming! When I first started to garden, I didn't want to spend years researching before I started, so I just jumped in and started. My mom has had a garden off and on and I started with the *little* I knew from helping her.

I did kind of "whatever" until 2015 when I read the book, *Teaming With Microbes,* by Lowenfels and Lewis.[1] It's my favorite gardening book. It explains how the microbes in the soil work to make and put the minerals and vitamins in the foods we grow and eat. Then it gives you basic guidelines on how to do it. In short, *Teaming With Microbes* explains how to grow a *'better than organic'* garden.

What Do I mean by "Better Than Organic"?

A garden that's better than organic is more than a garden "not sprayed with poison". It's a garden where the vegetables you eat are loaded with vitamins and minerals and they taste like they should taste.

You do this by starting with the soil. *Teaming with Microbes* made me **see** soil in another light. When I look at a handful of soil, I no longer see dirt. It's a world of living organisms who are living and dying...eating each other and being eaten...*breathing and alive!* It is

33

© Copyright 2017 | Julia Hubler | Soli Deo Gloria! *(Glory Be To God Alone!)*

just like your chickens, trees, milk kefir, or the bugs in your gut! God created atoms, molecules, and microbes in the soil to feed the plants and make them grow into healthy food for us to eat.

Once you learn how to care for the microbes in your soil, you'll have food with more of the nutrients, vitamins and minerals you need.

The first step is to stop looking at your soil as "dirt". Start seeing it as a bunch of live organisms that need to be cared for. You need to know what they need and how to treat them.

When garden soil is the first consideration, you're getting to the root of the matter. You're digging to the bottom of things and laying a firm foundation—a strong one you can build upon. Keeping the microbes in your soil alive and happy is how your grass, garden, orchard and entire homestead will be green and healthy. What do healthy microbes like?

Three Guidelines for the Microbial Conscious Gardener

Here are three recommendations for the microbial conscious gardener...

1. Get the right microbial ratio
2. Stop digging! Digging kills your microbes.
3. Mulch everything

1. Get the Right Microbial Ratio

Bacteria and fungi are valuable microbes in your soil. The remaining two points come back to this key issue. *What microbes do you need in the soil? Do you need a higher population of bacteria or fungi?* Understanding them and how they work is extremely important to a healthy garden.

The Microbe Balance—Bacteria and fungi are two amazing microbes in your soil. The key to healthy soil is finding the correct ratio between these two, so that you have the right balance for the right plants.

Bacteria and fungi are a great place to start. Truth be told, there are many more microbes and living organisms that need to be considered. Protozoa, nematodes, and archaea are all important too. I highly recommend reading the book, *Teaming With Microbes* to gain further knowledge. Borrow it from the library or buy it. It's worth every penny.

The type of microbes you want in your soil depends on whether you grow annuals or perennials. (Annuals are plants you replant every year. Most vegetables are annuals. Perennials are the ones you plant once, and they live for years. Fruit trees are berries and two great examples.)

Bacteria & Annuals—All of your annual plants grow best in bacteria-dominated soil. Annuals include: your vegetable garden, annual flowers, etc. They need a higher ratio of bacteria over fungi.

The reason annuals like bacteria is because of the form of nitrogen the bacterial soil supports. Bacterial soils have nitrogen in nitrate form. These nitrates are supported by bacteria and are what annuals need.

Fungi & Perennials—All of your perennial trees and shrubs thrive in a soil that's higher in fungi.

The reason for the fungal dominance required in perennial gardens is also the *form* of nitrogen. Only this time the perennials like their nitrogen in ammonium form, not in nitrates.

This may seem a bit confusing, but it's way simpler than the chemicals many gardeners use. *(Even if they are labeled "organic" or "natural.")*

Six Interesting Facts About Bacteria

1. Bacteria are single cell organisms. They reproduce by one cell dividing and turning into two cells. Each one does this again and again.
2. In laboratory conditions, one single cell bacterium can reproduce about 5 billion offspring in 12 hours.
3. There are more bacteria in the soil than any other living organism.
4. Bacteria… "are so minuscule that…250,000 to 500,000 of them can fit inside the period at the end of this sentence."[2]
5. They're a primary decomposer of organic matter.
6. Bacteria lock up nutrients in the soil by ingesting them. The nutrients then stay in the soil instead of being washed away like the chemical fertilizers.

Five Interesting Facts About Fungi

1. There are over 100,000 known fungi, and some say a million more are waiting to be discovered.
2. Besides the mushrooms and white threads in mulch, most other fungi are invisible, like bacteria.
3. Unlike bacteria, fungi hypha have the ability to grow in length, and they can grow to lengths measured by feet or meters.
4. A teaspoon of healthy soil may contain *several yards* of fungal hypha.
5. Fungi eat nematodes and retain the nutrients in themselves (the fungi), thus keeping the nutrients in the soil.

In points two and especially three we'll be discussing how you can grow soil with a higher bacteria or fungal population.

The concepts and principles behind bacteria and fungi can be complex...but the application is pretty easy. Fungi and bacteria are foundational to a healthy garden. They affect *when* to dig and *how* to mulch your garden.

Mushrooms popping up in your soil are a good sign of soil high in fungi. Don't eat them unless you know they're safe to eat. Many are poisonous but amazing for your fungal soils and trees. Consider mushrooms the "thumbs up" from your fungal microbes declaring, "You've got it right! We fungi are dominating the bacteria!"

2. Stop Digging

When you dig up your garden every season, you're killing your microbes. The first thing a microbial conscious gardener needs to do is stop!

There is a time when it's okay to dig up your garden. It's rare—only under certain conditions—and **not** every season. *Teaming With Microbes* explains it in detail. Basically, you dig or turn your garden if you have a high fungi to bacteria ratio in your annual garden.

When you dig your garden, it breaks up the long chains of fungi and opens the soil up to the bacteria. Doing it every year though will cause unnecessary killing of all your microbes.

Tilling in History

When people came to America, they cleared the forests (fungal soils) and dug their gardens before planting. This let in more bacteria. You don't need to do this every year. You're killing microbes when you dig. If the purpose is to change the fungal to bacteria ratio, that's okay, but there's no reason to unnecessarily kill off the microbes.

(One great bonus with this method is there's less unnecessary work! *Yay!*)

3. Mulch Everything

Last but not least, you need to mulch everything! The only way you are going to be able to garden with the right ratio of bacteria to fungi, without digging, is with mulch.

The Benefits of Mulch—Bare soil is a no-no! When you leave soil bare, you expose it to harsh elements such as the sun, cold, and more.

Quick Tip: Use Holistic Mulch
Note: I'm not taking about plastic mulch. Rocks aren't the best either. Neither of these add organic matter to the soil and therefore aren't feeding your microbes. They're not of any great long-term benefit to your soil or plants.

God designed native plants to drop leaves and sticks—to give mulch to cover the soil. Even in the desert, you'll find bits of dead leaves and sticks under the trees and shrubs.

When caring for soil, you always want it covered in mulch. There are several important things mulch does that make it a must:

- Mulch protects the soil and microbes from the harsh environment. The summer sun and heat are shaded out. The soil is kept warm during ice and cold. Mulch is an insulator and protector of soil life.
- Mulch prevents soil compaction.
- Mulch *reduces evaporation* and *absorbs more water*. It later releases that water into the soil when it's needed.
- Living organisms in mulch and the top few inches of soil purify greywater very effectively. *(See Chapter 12)*
- Mulch is great for natural weed control. *(See Chapter 10.)*
- It looks a lot neater to have your soils mulched.
- Mulch encourages a diversity of life in your soils!

What Kind of Mulch Do I Use?—The type of mulch you use will vary, depending on the kind of soil you're aiming for. Bacteria and fungi each grow best with different kinds of mulch.

Bacteria prefer small, ground-up, and wet mulches.
Mulch Suggestions For Bacterial Soil:
- Straw and hay—It's best not to use Bermuda hay in the garden. More about this in a minute.
- Alfalfa
- Fresh grass clippings—Don't apply too thickly or it may go anaerobic. It would smell and be bad for the microbes you want to promote.
- Small, ground or chopped-up annual plants after harvest—For example: after your growing season chop up your dead squash, watermelon, and lettuce plants and put them back on your garden as mulch.
- Brown leaves that have been ground into very fine pieces
- Bacterial compost

Fungi like coarse, large, hard, and drier mulches.
Mulch Suggestions For Fungal Soil:
- Aged wood chips and bark (avoid cedar chips)
- Whole brown leaves
- Aged pine needles
- Fungal compost

> **Quick Tip: Age Your Wood Chips**
> Make sure you age your wood chips before you apply them to your trees. If you add the fresh, brand-new chips onto your soil, you are most likely going to have the new chips stealing nitrogen from your soil and your tree. It can even kill the tree! You don't want that. So after getting your wood chips, let them sit for a year and then use them freely—*Simple!*

How to Mulch—You mulch differently based on what ratio of bacteria to fungi you want in the soil. Either way, here is one rule that applies to both fungal and bacterial soils:

Don't use too much mulch! You can suffocate the microbes. The microbes in the soil need oxygen. *Teaming With Microbes* recommends 2-3 inches of mulch on the soil. Any more than this and you risk smothering the microbes in the soil. After the first application, the mulch will settle down quickly. You can later add more so you always have 2-3 inches of mulch on your soil.

How to Mulch for Fungi—Always lay fungal mulch **on top** of the soil. This encourages a fungal dominance in the soil. *Never mix fungal mulch in the soil!*

How to Mulch for Bacteria—*Teaming With Microbes* recommends working bacterial mulches into the top couple inches of soil. Just to be safe, I usually leave my bacterial mulches on top of the soil. Either way, make sure you use a bacterial mulch and not fungal mulch if you mix it in and only mix it in the top one or two inches—never deeper than that.

As a general rule, bacterial mulches are more balanced in the nitrogen to carbon ratio, and shouldn't tie up the nitrogen. If in doubt, lay the mulch on top.

Bermuda Hay & the Garden—Keep Bermuda out of the garden at all costs!
When Bermuda gets in the garden, the roots are *extremely invasive* and can take over an entire garden. It is recommended not to mulch with Bermuda hay because the hay may contain seeds that will germinate in your garden, and then you'll have an up-hill battle. Play it safe and keep the Bermuda away from the garden. *(Use it to mulch your pasture or orchard trees instead.)*

Grass clippings can also pose this problem if you're letting them grow long and then cutting and putting that on your garden. The seeds will develop when it gets tall and you'll spread those in your garden. With short-kept lawn clippings you *may* not have the seed problem.

Quick Tip: Mulch & Compost

"Mulches excel when they are used in conjunction with compost. Put the compost down first and then cover with mulch…the compost organisms will inoculate the mulch, and begin to decay it as well." —*Teaming With Microbes*[3]

Compost as Mulch—Both fungal and bacterial soils *thrive* with compost. All good
composts have tons of living fungi and bacteria. Applying compost with the right ratio of fungi and bacteria to the right soils boosts either the fungal or bacterial populations.

It's best to apply the correct type of compost to the correct soil type. The compost with more fungi goes under fruit trees. The compost with more bacteria goes in the vegetable and annual gardens.

By applying the right kind of microbes in the right place, you help establish a higher bacterial or fungal ratio in the correct soils.

How do you make compost with a higher ratio of fungi or a higher ratio of bacteria? I'll leave that for the next chapter.

Mulching Grass

If may sound funny to "mulch grass." If you're used to mulching your garden, you're probably thinking, "How do you mulch grass!?" It's simple. If you're planting, after you sow the seed (Optionally, put down compost or manure first—before you sow the seeds—for a natural nitrogen and microbes boost.) cover the seeds with 2-3 inches of mulch. (It'll shrink down after it settles. You can add some more, just don't have more than 2-3" over the soil.) Mulch gives the microbes protection before the grass is established. Then the grass takes over and provides protection to the microbes.

If your pasture is growing, there are two ways you can mulch. 1. When the grass is long, cut or mow it and lay it back on the soil as mulch. 2. After the cow (or sheep) eats the grass down, put down a few inches of straw. The new grass will grow through it.

(When choosing mulch for your grass, stick with straw, hay or compost.)

Microbes & Your Grass

Much of the above discussion on microbes was more specifically related to your garden and orchard. Let's see how the grass and rotational grazing laid out in the last chapter work with the microbes in your pasture. Everything we talked about in that chapter ended up relating to the microbes.

Multiple Species on your pasture means diversity, which is important to healthy microbes. This diversity of species means…

More Kinds of Herbage Will Be Eaten Each kind of animal prefers to eat different herbage and grasses. When put together, they eat more of everything and they eat it differently. When using a combination of animals, more of the grass will be eaten. (The cows get the long grass and the sheep mow it short.) This causes the healthy, natural life-and-death cycle of the plants and roots, which promotes strong microbes.

Chickens help break down and spread the manure. This makes it easier for the microbes to digest and feed the plant's roots. The chickens also eat the bad bugs, which is good for the good microbes.

Parasites & Nutrients in the manure are different. This means more healthy diversity for the microbes and less of the bad bugs (parasites).

Rotational grazing with multiple species is the key to healthy microbes in the pasture.

Chapter 6: Compost—A Homesteader's Best Friend...

Compost is an important piece to the homestead puzzle. The goal is to find a connection, a place you can plug the "not needed" leftovers into. There shouldn't be waste. If something is wasted, this is a sign you've got a piece missing—a gap you need to fill in. Composting makes hundreds of connections!

Most things don't need to be thrown in the landfill. Homesteaders need all that "trash" but don't view it as trash. Look at it as an ingredient for the compost pile. Then see all the ways you can use this amazing ingredient.

Amazing Benefits of Compost

To any healthy garden, pasture, or orchard, compost is the **best** food.

Compost:
- Builds your soil's fertility
- Increases the microbial activity in your soil
- Increases moisture retention and drainage
- Provides organic matter

Compost is way better than it's substitute—peat moss. There are no microbes in peat moss, only organic matter. Organic matter is important, but mostly so it can support healthy, living microbes. We, on occasion, will use peat moss to start seeds, but compost is *exceptionally* better to use in your garden.

Compost makes your:

- Plants thrive and look better
- Fruits and vegetables contain more minerals and vitamins
- Fruits and vegetables taste better
- Organic matter act like a sponge and more rainwater will infiltrate into your soil when it rains
- Landscape look prettier—rich healthy soil and healthy plants look more beautiful.

Compost is the *best* natural plant food. If there is only *one* thing you do for your garden, pasture and trees, give them compost. The organic matter, nitrogen, and microbes are the best thing you can give your soil.

Compost & Rainwater

Organic matter (mulch, wood chips, straw, manure, compost, etc.) on top of and in your soil is amazing. One of the things it does is to make the soil better able to absorb the water when it rains. Instead of the water running over the soil, it seeps in. The organic matter acts like a sponge, soaking up and holding water. Over time it releases the water into the soil where it's needed.

Compost is a Waste Solution

Compost provides a use for tons of little odds and ends you'd otherwise waste. There are so many things you can compost. Any organic matter, plants, food scraps, kitchen scraps, and manure can be turned into microbe-rich food for your soil.

Everyone thinks that throwing things away is no big deal. What about the landfill it's going to and the cost you pay to get it there? Compost is a better solution. In the end, instead of paying for it, you get paid. You can even sell compost if you want. Otherwise, you use the high quality stuff for your fruits and vegetables.

Compost is a Money Saver

When you compost most of your "trash" there isn't much left for the trash man. You can burn the rest if legally allowed to or take it to a landfill yourself to save money on the trash bill. *It costs money to waste things.*

Vermicomposting for Small Spaces

Even if you live in a tiny house with no yard, you can still compost. Vermicomposting *(composting with earthworms)* is great for situations with little space. I've wanted to try vermicomposting, but we have lots of land and so it hasn't made it to the top of our list yet.

There are lots of great "how-to's" online. The basic idea is to have earth worms in a bucket or bin with bedding (newspaper is a common material used). Then you feed them your food scraps. As long as it's done correctly, it shouldn't smell.

The great thing is that you can do it right under your kitchen sink. If you're limited on space, I highly recommend looking into this composting method.

If you haven't realized it yet, the homestead *needs* compost—as much as you can make!

Composting doesn't need to be intense. There's a composting method called lazy, slow or cold-composting. You'll still get the long-term benefits as with the quicker compost.

Compost is Teaming With Life!

A *teaspoon* of compost contains:
1. 400-900 feet of fungal hyphae
2. Up to a billion bacteria
3. 10,000-50,000 protozoa
4. 30-300 nematodes

When it comes to a microbial count, even the best garden soil doesn't stand a chance when compared to compost.

Making Compost:

Compost Basics—The basic recipe for compost is simple. It's a ratio between carbon and nitrogen—C:N. The right C:N ratio is about 25:1 to 30:1. There are compost calculators online to help you figure out how much of each you need to get the right ratio.

You can use any organic matter—leaves, manure, straw, wood chips, kitchen scraps, etc.—as long as you get the right C:N ratio.

The other two things you need to consider are air and water. You want the compost to be moist but not sopping. A good guideline is that it should be moist like a wrung out sponge.

Air is also key. The lack of air can cause bad smells. Turning the pile every so often is a great way to achieve good air flow. *(Or have the chickens do it.)*

Bacterial vs. Fungal Compost—There are thousands of methods you can use to compost. The bigger question is—*what do you want in the finished product?*

We talked about bacteria and fungi in the last chapter. I ended by pointing out that you want the same kind of microbes in the compost that you want in the soil.

Apply compost with a higher fungal population to the perennials, orchard, shrubs, etc. Give the compost with more bacteria to your annuals and vegetable garden.

Establishing the Right Microbes in Your Compost—The ingredients you use to establish the C:N ratio is what determines the bacteria over fungal count (and visa-versa). When you hear about composting, a lot of times the materials will be divided into brown and green.

Brown organic matter (like leaves, bark, and wood chips) support the fungi and are high in carbon. The green organic matter (like grass clippings, kitchen scraps, fresh-picked weeds, etc.) are higher in nitrogen and support bacteria.

To get the right C:N ratio, most of the time you'll use both green and brown materials. Keep this in mind: bacteria like the small, sugary, wetter organic matter. Fungi like the larger, coarser, drier organic matter.

After you've decided what kind of compost you want to make, use as many as you can of it's (bacteria or fungi's) favorite "foods," while still keeping the C:N ratio.

How to Make Compost With Chickens

Chickens are great for the compost pile. Both chickens and compost benefit when working together.

When chickens are given access to a compost pile they:
- Scratch and tear it down—providing oxygen which a compost pile needs.
- Eat out the bugs, grubs or larvae they find—things you don't want in the garden.
- Leave behind their manure, which adds a little extra nitrogen to the pile.

I've seen great chicken-composting systems designed for the small-scale homesteader—simple systems. You start a new compost pile every week and turn all the piles you have going from the last few weeks. When a pile is done, off it goes to the garden.

Throughout the week you add your vegetable scraps to the top of the last pile—your newest pile. The chickens eat what they want and the rest decomposes. Nothing is wasted. You have compost for your garden, and you can cut your chickens' feed bill. Instead of paying for their feed, you go even farther and make money from the compost by either using it in your garden or selling it. The compost feeds the chickens—the chickens work and feed the compost.

Chapter 7: The Orchard & Fruit Tree Guilds...

Trees are valuable on the homestead. It'd be nice to start a homestead with several large fruit and shade trees. Sorry to say, it rarely works like that.

Trees Are Essential

"When's the best time to plant a tree?" 50 years ago? 20? 10?

I've heard different numbers. Either way, we've got some catching up to do! Plant your trees as soon as possible.

Trees take a long time to get going—*so start now!* Grow as many as you can. They're a wonderful long-term investment.

An Orchard or Guilds?

When I think of an orchard, I picture the big farm orchards—bunches of trees, planted in perfect straight rows. The trees are fed chemical fertilizers, nitrogen, pesticides, weed killers and everything else they *"need"*.

After researching, I've realized it's better to plant trees in guilds. A guild is when you have a tree growing in the center of other plants, shrubs, flowers and herbs. A guild is far closer to a self-sustaining system than a typical orchard.

The Amazing Benefits of Guilds—The sustainability of guilds is amazing! The diversity of life supports itself way better than the standard orchard. Instead of the harmful fertilizers, nitrogen, pesticides, and weed killers; the diverse life in a guild provides these basic elements more naturally.

The plants and life you grow in a guild do the following:
- They fix nitrogen, making it available for the tree and other plants.
- Some plants with a deep taproot mine up minerals from deep in the soil and make them accessible to neighboring plants.
- Herbs act as natural pesticides, keeping bad bugs away and also attracting the good bugs.
- Flowers bring pollinators.
- Plants can be grown, chopped, and laid back on the soil as mulch.
- The mulch keeps the weeds at bay and also supports the microbes in the soil.
- The fowl provide fertilizer and pest control.

Guilds have a beautiful, healthy, diversity of life! They are hardier and more robust than any monoculture orchard. They are a great pick for the holistic homestead.

What's in a Guild?

"Guild" is a great permaculture term. Guilds are designed to take care of themselves with little to no help from outside sources such as fertilizers, pesticides, or even after established—compost and mulch.

Here's a look at all the parts that go into a guild. Every guild will look different. Some of your guilds may have all of these pieces and others may only have a few. That's fine. Just remember, *the more diversity the better and healthier the guild.*

The Center Tree—Any kind of tree can be at the center of a guild. The center tree provides shade and shelter for the lower plants. Apple, pecan, lemon—any tree will work.

When you pick the tree and other plants to grow around it you need to keep your whole guild in mind. Pick plants with similar water needs. You don't want to plant a thirsty swamp tree with a desert cactus.

Nitrogen Fixers—Plants which fix nitrogen in the soil provide nitrogen in the right form for the other plants in the guild. Most legumes fix nitrogen into the soil. They are important to your guild.

Herbs & Flowers—Herbs and flowers keep the bad bugs away and attract beneficial insects, which pollinate your trees. Herbs like rosemary and lavender repel rabbits.

Beneficial Insects & Pollinators—Beneficial insects eat the bad bugs which destroy fruit and trees. They also pollinate the flowers in the guild.

> ### Native Trees & Nitrogen
> Native trees can be good for other trees in your guilds. Most legumes fix nitrogen in the soil. This means the neighboring plants and trees can get nitrogen in the right form, and absorb it.
> A lot of native trees are legumes. In Arizona the Mesquite and Palo Verde are legumes. Do a quick google search and find out which trees in your area are legumes. Incorporate a number of them in your fruit guilds.

Small Trees & Shrubs—Small trees and/or shrubs are great to plant under your center tree. These may be fruit-producing, like pomegranates, grapes, berries, etc., or they can be nitrogen fixing like the Siberian Pea Shrub.

Ground Cover—A ground cover helps keep the weeds down. A legume like clover will also fix nitrogen in the soil. Buckwheat is another excellent ground cover. It isn't a legume, but it grows quickly and provides great organic matter for the soil.

Deep Rooted Plants—Dandelions and comfrey are a great place to start! Both draw up minerals from deep down in the soil so neighboring plants can use them. You can also use dandelions and especially comfrey as chop and drop mulch.

> ### Quick Tip: Chop & Drop Mulch...
> Chop & drop mulch is as easy as it sounds. Grow dandelions or comfrey (for example), and when they've grown tall, chop them right above the soil line and lay them on the soil as mulch.

Wood Chips, Compost & Mulch—Mulch on the soil is important for healthy microbes. Aged wood chips are great in a perennial, fungal dominant guild. Keep a few inches of mulch over the soil at all times.

Chickens & Animals—Chickens and other fowl are good to have roaming around your guilds. They'll eat dropped fruit off the ground, which will keep diseases and bad bugs away from your trees and plants. They also are great with insect control.

Don't forget to feed apple tree trimmings to your goats! *(See page 107)*

Microbes—Microbes love the diversity of life in guilds! Mulch and diversity of plant and animal life are important for strong, healthy microbes.

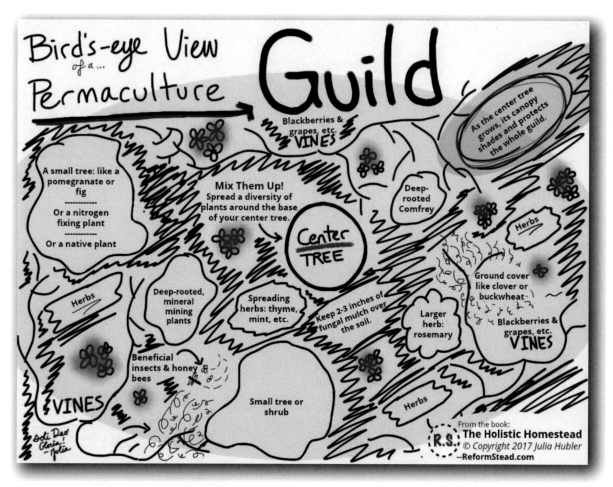

How to Plant a Guild

Guilds are easy to grow on the homestead. Collect a combination of different seeds and transplants as listed above and plant them around the center tree.

You can plant them all at the same time. You don't need to plant one and wait to plant another.

Add lots of compost and mulch when you're starting a guild. Taken to its fullest, guilds can grow their own mulch and fertilizers through plants and sometimes fowl. However, it's best to give them a boost to get them started.

If you've already planted your trees and want to turn them into guilds, plant transplants and seeds of all the other species around the base of the center tree. Plant them all at once if you want, or do it over time.

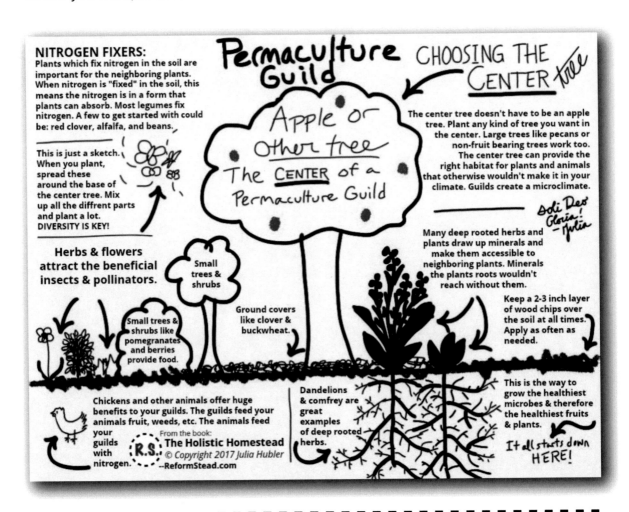

NITROGEN FIXERS:
Plants which fix nitrogen in the soil are important for the neighboring plants. When nitrogen is "fixed" in the soil, this means the nitrogen is in a form that plants can absorb. Most legumes fix nitrogen. A few to get started with could be: red clover, alfalfa, and beans.

This is just a sketch. When you plant, spread these around the base of the center tree. Mix up all the diffrent parts and plant a lot. DIVERSITY IS KEY!

Herbs & flowers attract the beneficial insects & pollinators.

Small trees & shrubs like pomegranates and berries provide food.

Small trees & shrubs

Ground covers like clover & buckwheat.

Permaculture Guild

Apple or other tree

The CENTER of a Permaculture Guild

CHOOSING THE CENTER tree

The center tree doesn't have to be an apple tree. Plant any kind of tree you want in the center. Large trees like pecans or non-fruit bearing trees work too. The center tree can provide the right habitat for plants and animals that otherwise wouldn't make it in your climate. Guilds create a microclimate.

Soli Deo Gloria! —Julia

Many deep rooted herbs and plants draw up minerals and make them accessible to neighboring plants. Minerals the plants roots wouldn't reach without them.

Keep a 2-3 inch layer of wood chips over the soil at all times. Apply as often as needed.

Chickens and other animals offer huge benefits to your guilds. The guilds feed your animals fruit, weeds, etc. The animals feed your guilds with nitrogen.

From the book:
R.S. The Holistic Homestead
© Copyright 2017 Julia Hubler
--ReformStead.com

Dandelions & comfrey are great examples of deep rooted herbs.

This is the way to grow the healthiest microbes & therefore the healthiest fruits & plants.

It all starts down HERE!

Better Than Organic!
"Just because certain practices are acceptable under federal standards doesn't mean they are healthy for the orchard as a whole. So-called deep organics goes beyond substituting natural materials for synthetic chemicals and recognizes that ecosystem dynamics are best supported by prioritizing soil health." —*The Holistic Orchard*[1]

Guild Examples From Our Homestead:

Here are a few examples of guilds on our homestead. Not all of them are where I'd like them to be because we planted most of our trees before I learned of guilds. On the side you'll see a "things to add" list. Those are ideas of things we're gradually adding into our guilds.

Grass in the Orchard & Guilds...

Everyone likes to grow grass in the orchard and keep it mowed short. (Like they do in the monoculture farms.) This is not healthy for the trees. A little grass mixed in with the other plants around the tree is okay. Just *don't* keep it mowed short. It's best to let it grow very long and then be chop it down.

The reason for this is the way the grass roots grow. When grass is constantly mowed short, the roots grow like a thick mat. This cuts off the room the tree roots need and is bad for the health of the tree.

When the grass is allowed to grow long and is cut short only a few times a year, the roots grow differently. They grow thin, long and deep. This is fine for the tree as its roots will grow in and around the grass roots.

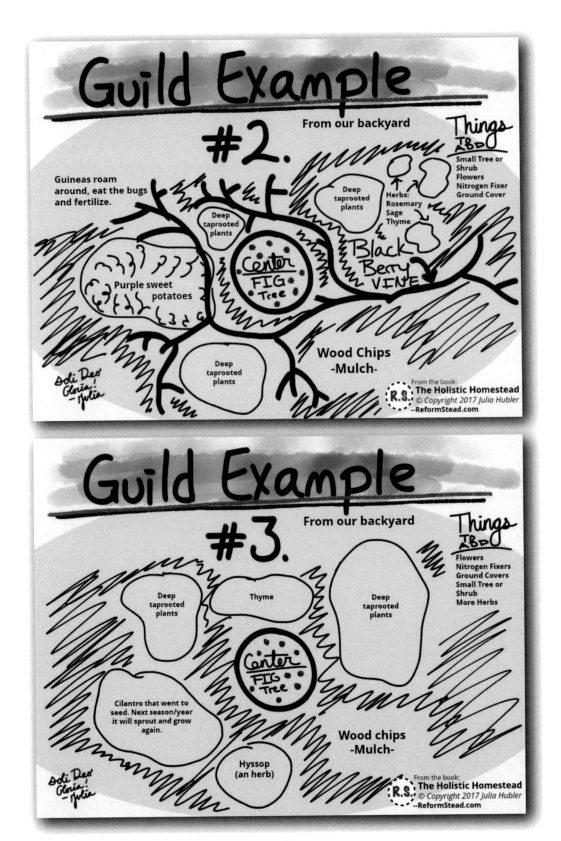

Guild Example

#2.

From our backyard

Things TBD
Small Tree or Shrub
Flowers
Nitrogen Fixer
Ground Cover

Guineas roam around, eat the bugs and fertilize.

Deep taprooted plants

Deep taprooted plants

Herbs: Rosemary Sage Thyme

Center FIG Tree

Purple sweet potatoes

Black Berry VINE

Deep taprooted plants

Wood Chips -Mulch-

Soli Deo Gloria! -Julia

From the book:
The Holistic Homestead
© Copyright 2017 Julia Hubler
--ReformStead.com

Guild Example

#3.

From our backyard

Things TBD
Flowers
Nitrogen Fixers
Ground Covers
Small Tree or Shrub
More Herbs

Deep taprooted plants

Thyme

Deep taprooted plants

Center FIG Tree

Cilantro that went to seed. Next season/year it will sprout and grow again.

Hyssop (an herb)

Wood chips -Mulch-

Soli Deo Gloria! -Julia

From the book:
The Holistic Homestead
© Copyright 2017 Julia Hubler
--ReformStead.com

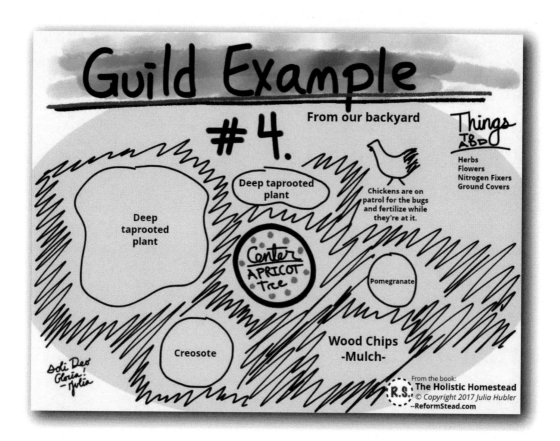

Guild Example

From our backyard

#4.

Things TBD
- Herbs
- Flowers
- Nitrogen Fixers
- Ground Covers

Deep taprooted plant

Deep taprooted plant

Chickens are on patrol for the bugs and fertilize while they're at it.

Center APRICOT Tree

Pomegranate

Creosote

Wood Chips -Mulch-

Soli Deo Gloria! -Julia

From the book:
The Holistic Homestead
© Copyright 2017 Julia Hubler
--ReformStead.com

55

Chapter 8: Holistic Vegetable Gardening...

Organic vegetables grown in your garden are a wonderful piece of your homestead's puzzle and vegetable gardening is one thing most homesteaders will be doing a lot of. Growing your own vegetables means you have control over the soil. Therefore, your vegetables can contain more minerals, vitamins and nutrients than store-bought produce.

As mentioned in previous chapters, strong healthy microbes are the key to growing produce with the most nutrients and minerals. In earlier chapters we laid the groundwork by learning how to achieve and grow a healthy population of microbes in your soil.

Now let's talk about how to think holistically on a few practical issues you'll confront while setting up your garden. Some of them you may already know about, but others may be new to you. As in the rest of this book, we're going beyond the basics. You can find the simple basics in any of the *Storey's* homesteading books. *(See Resources Chapter, page 192.)* Let's think holistically.

Raised Beds, Ground Level, or Sunken Beds

When it comes to planting there are three basic ways you can proceed. All methods have their pros and cons. You can plant in:

1.   Raised beds

2. Ground level
3. Sunken beds

1. Raised Beds—Raised beds make cute, neat little gardens. They can look beautiful and be done nicely. Raised beds are great if you want a slightly easier job, since being able to sit and work up high can be easier on your back and legs.

Another great thing about raised beds is you get to start with good soil. When we made ours, we used 100% compost. The plants we grew in there loved it—especially the deep root vegetables.

One of the downsides with raised beds is that they cost money to build. They can be done cheaply and still look nice if you try, but this will take effort. You can use things you find laying around or someone else's unneeded materials. Otherwise, you can end up spending quite a bit on them.

The biggest problem we've had with raised beds is water! We set up lots of raised beds and had great winter gardens. (Yes, wintertime here is like most of the country's spring. Winter is our best gardening season in Phoenix, Arizona.) When it started to get hot, forget it! We watered with the hose and it was nearly impossible to keep enough water in the raised beds. The poor plants were soon cooked. We might have been able to get it to work if we had set up an automatic watering system, but they still need way more water than the following methods. It's not worth the extra money required for the additional water in such a hot, dry climate.

2. Ground Level—This method requires much less water. It's better adapted to infrequent, long, and deep waterings, which are important—especially in the desert. (And everywhere else too.) Mulch, of course, helps keep even more water in the soil and reduces evaporation.

3. Sunken Beds—After trying the raised beds and ground level gardening, this method was looking better and better to us. You save water going from the raised beds to ground level gardening, so it makes sense it would only get better by going one step further. It also fits with rainwater and greywater harvesting.

With sunken beds instead of raising the soil, or gardening at ground level, you actually dig soil out and make your garden bed a few to several inches lower than the soil was naturally. This causes water to collect there instead of running away.

I've read a good bit about this method and have been pleased with the results I've had the few times I've tried it. It really made a difference. When you start with soil that's been moved and constructed in a way that collects water, the soil absorbs it better and there's less run-off. It's great for areas where water is scarce and valuable.

> **It's More Than a Good Watering System**
> Consider the landscape of the soil before planting. You can have a great automatic watering system and waste a lot of water if it's not soaking in the soil because it's running away or evaporating.
>
> Is your garden soil designed in a way to promote water run-off or water infiltration?

Which is Best Suited to Your Climate?

Consider your water needs. Is water scarce? Do you need to water often or just on occasion? If you have too much water and trouble keeping plants dry enough, raised beds may be a great option. If you live in the desert, growing sunken beds is the most water-wise technique.

The Best Answer to Many Garden Problems

There's one simple key to a healthy garden. Unfortunately, there'll still be problems and pests that will come up and you'll need to deal with them. The long-term answer though, to a garden with fewer problems is...

Healthy Microbes!

Pests & Diseases in a Microbe Garden

The pests and diseases people worry about in their gardens are greatly reduced, if not totally kept away, with a healthy population of microbes. When the microbes are working together properly, their lifecycle keeps the garden healthy and free of diseases and uncontrollable pests.

With microbial conscious gardening, another

> **Quick Tip: Planting, Timing & Extending the Harvest**
> Timing can be everything for a garden. Our garden always grows best when we get it in as early as possible. Planting often and as long as you can also extends the harvest season. Do your big planting early and then keep planting seeds every week or two. We did this last year and had a much longer harvest time.

thing you need to worry about less is crop rotation. Crop rotation is essential when you're tilling every year and destroying and killing the microbes, fungi and bacteria. Killing them means they have to start over and repopulate the soil. When you stop tilling, the microbes grow strong and are better able to fight off bad bugs and diseases.

I love the straightforwardness of this gardening method. It's way easier to use basic things like mulch and compost, than to figure out all the chemical solutions, "natural" or not, for pests and diseases.

Companion Planting or Monoculture—Microbes Again!

Although crop rotation is no longer essential, companion planting is. When you grow your plants and vegetables together, you are further encouraging a healthy diversity of life.

The monoculture farms are not a good example for a homesteader to follow. Monoculture farms require lots of chemicals in the form of fertilizers, pesticides and herbicides. There's no reason to use these on the homestead! Furthermore, there's no reason to take their practices as a pattern and have a mini monoculture-farm in your backyard. Free yourself from that and see the natural options—like companion planting.

A great common example of companion planting can be learned from the Native Americans. They taught the Pilgrims to plant corn when they moved to America. First, they put a fish in the bottom of the hole (natural fertilizer), then they added the corn seed. Right around it they planted squash and/or melons and beans. The beans would grow up the corn stalk as it grew and fix the nitrogen in the soil. Squash and melons were a natural "live mulch" to shade the soil and prevent evaporation for the corn. This is one example that's often talked about in gardening circles, and it's so amazing it'll never grow old.

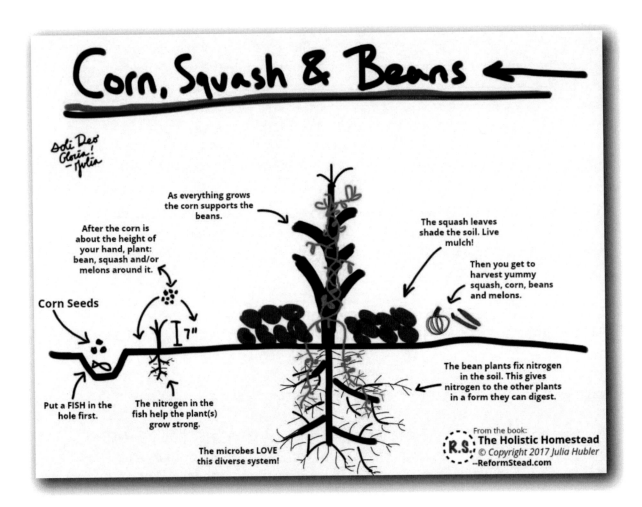

Corn, Squash & Beans ←

Soli Deo Gloria! —Julia

As everything grows the corn supports the beans.

After the corn is about the height of your hand, plant: bean, squash and/or melons around it.

Corn Seeds

7"

Put a FISH in the hole first.

The nitrogen in the fish help the plant(s) grow strong.

The squash leaves shade the soil. Live mulch!

Then you get to harvest yummy squash, corn, beans and melons.

The bean plants fix nitrogen in the soil. This gives nitrogen to the other plants in a form they can digest.

The microbes LOVE this diverse system!

From the book:
The Holistic Homestead
© Copyright 2017 Julia Hubler
--ReformStead.com
R.S.

Straight Rows or Not?

Is it good to plant in straight rows? I'll leave the final answer up to you. One thing I've noticed though is how much better everything grows when it is just slightly squeezed together in an uneven pattern. (Notice I said "slightly squeezed." When you don't plant in perfectly straight rows you are able to get a lot more plants in the same amount of space. Don't skip thinning your plants. They won't grow as big, or even be able to reach full maturity if not given adequate room.)

Circle gardens are also fun! We have a garden planted in a big spiral and I think it looks better than the rows.

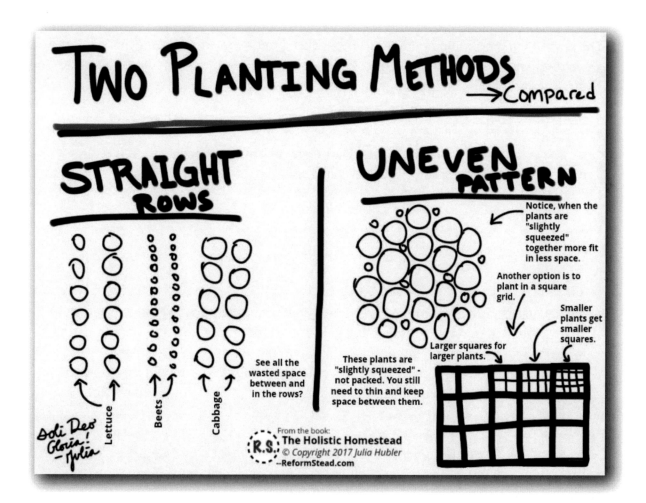

Annual Vegetable Gardening

Growing annuals is great for a holistic homestead. Annuals grow fast and before you know it, you have healthy vegetables on the dinner table.

There are so many different kinds of vegetables you can try! It's fun to try them all and see which ones do well in your climate or which ones are your family's favorites. Annuals are great! Squash, beans, lettuce and watermelons are wonderful on the homestead.

Perennial Vegetables

I've yet to grow perennial vegetables. Some are the simple and common vegetables like asparagus and artichokes. There are also so many others that are more rare. Some of them look interesting, and I wonder what they taste like.

The reason I'm mentioning perennials is because I think they may be another valuable piece to the homestead puzzle. I'm looking forward to branching out into perennials. They're worth looking into for your homestead. *(See Resources Chapter, page 192.)*

(See Resources Chapter, page 192.)

Quick Tip: Harvest for Your Family First

When you plant a chicken garden, all the fruits and vegetables you raise obviously don't have to go to your chickens—especially with fruit trees. Harvest as much as you can for your family. Then, what you miss will fall for the chickens to eat.

Gardening for Chickens

A chicken garden is a great food source for your chickens. A chicken garden does more than provide food for your chickens. It'll give your birds shade from the harsh sun and a safe hiding place from aerial predators. It'll also make your homestead more beautiful and keep the microbes in the soil around your coop healthy. Gardening for chickens can cut your feed bill and provide a healthy, beautiful and cool (the cold kind of cool) habitat for them to live in.

By growing your own chicken food, you're adding to your list of home-grown food sources, while at the same time cutting back on feed expenses and saving money.

Learn to See: Messy Trees Are Great!

Messy fruit trees are great for planting by your chicken's coop. Take the mulberry for example. Mulberries are huge trees, but they give lots of shade and fruit. Mulberries are know to be quite messy. When they drop their fruit, it stains concrete and leaves a mess wherever they are. All those drawbacks are assets when a mulberry tree is near your chicken coop. Plant a big tree with lots of shade for your coop which will keep it cool in the sweltering, hot, summer afternoons. Then the trees make a mess where the chickens are. The chickens get to eat the fruit, saving you money on your feed bill, and they keep everything neat and tidy. We've just used holistic thinking and permaculture to turn a problem into a solution!

Two Methods for Feeding Your Chickens Fresh Produce

There are two basic ways you can garden for your chickens:

1. Cut and carry vegetables from your garden to the chickens.
2. Grow a garden specifically for them.

Better yet, do a little of both. You can cut and carry produce to your flock while you're setting up a chicken garden. The main goal is to feed them fresh vegetables and greens from your garden.

The nice thing about having a garden that's right there all the time for the chickens is you save time and effort. Instead of harvesting and bringing it to them, they can harvest what they want.

Chickens & Destruction in the Garden

If you're a gardener and own chickens, you are probably thinking I'm crazy! Without careful consideration and planning, a chicken can be the most destructive monster to the garden. You need to protect the plants and seedlings while they are young. If you don't, your chicken garden will be a flop. With the proper care, you can get the plants to mature enough so the chickens won't destroy them.

What to Plant for Your Chickens

If you'll eat it, so will they—greens, meat, fat, broth, fruit, nuts and seeds, etc. *(With the exception of foods that can be dangerous to them like chocolate, avocados and some say citrus—although we haven't had any problems with feeding it.)*

When it comes to what to plant, the list is nearly endless! As with your vegetable garden, you'll want to make sure the plants or trees grow in your area before you plant them. Plants especially great for chickens are: mulberries, stinging nettle, squash, lettuce, kale and sunflowers—just to name a few. There's a chart that has a list of great foods you can grow for chickens in the Appendix. *(See page 211)*

When you decide what to plant, there are a few things to think about:
• How long does the plant live?
• Is it a perennial or an annual? Perennials live for years. Consider them an investment in the future. Annuals live for a short time and die. They are better for short-term solutions.
• How big is it going to get? Remember trees provide shade, so place them in such a way so that you're using that to your advantage.
• Is the plant invasive? Good to know before you plant so that you can have a plan so it doesn't take over your whole garden.

- How many years is the plant going to be producing food? Similar question to the perennial vs. annual.
- Is the plant giving the chickens more than food? Is it giving food, shade, healing or health benefits (herbs)?
- What other benefits are my chickens going to get from this plant? Plant so they are helping in as many ways as possible. If a tree provides shade and your coop gets too much sun, plant the tree to block the sun.
- How can I plant so I'm solving another problem too?

When you are planting a holistic chicken garden, you want to have diversity. You want as many species as possible. Permaculture guilds would be a great addition to a chicken garden.

***Note: There are some inedible landscape plants which are poisonous to chickens. On the holistic homestead, I can't see why you'd bother planting them anyway. Do a quick google search to be sure you are planting chicken-safe plants.

Structures to Protect Young Plants & Seeds

Protecting new seeds and plants is important to the success of your chicken garden. Even a 5-ft tall, newly planted tree could be at risk of destruction by your chickens if not protected. You need to do two things:

1. Keep the chickens from eating the leaves and stems of the plants.
2. Keep them from digging up the roots.

The easiest way to do this is to use chicken wire around each individual plant and tree. When you do this, make sure they can't get through, under, or over the chicken wire.

Perennials are especially important to protect. You're *investing* in them so they'll give lots of food for years. With annuals it's not as big a deal if the chickens break in and eat your seedlings. Not that you'd want them to, but the perennials are more important.

It's work to make secure fences, and it can be a tedious job. Do it right the first time and you won't be sorry.

Here's one way to protect young plants from chickens. (1) I have two stakes in the ground, (2) with chicken wire *(it's hard to see in the picture)* that is secured on all sides including the (3) top and bottom. (4) The bottom is secured with two cinder blocks. The chicken wire is tied to the fence with hay twine.

How to Protect a new tree from chickens.

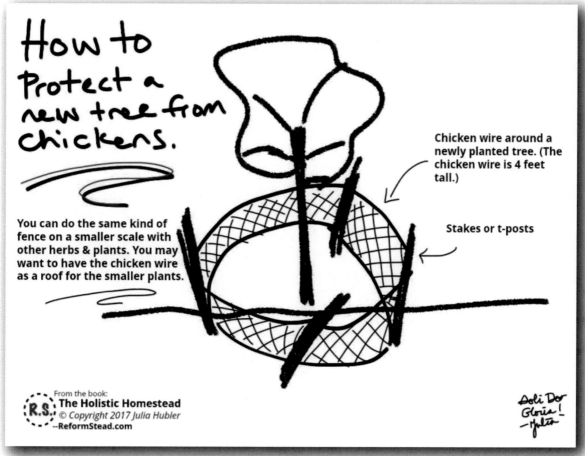

Chicken wire around a newly planted tree. (The chicken wire is 4 feet tall.)

Stakes or t-posts

You can do the same kind of fence on a smaller scale with other herbs & plants. You may want to have the chicken wire as a roof for the smaller plants.

From the book:
The Holistic Homestead
© Copyright 2017 Julia Hubler
–ReformStead.com

Soli Deo Gloria!
–Julia

Holistic Seeds & Seed Saving—Simplified

Buying seeds can get confusing. To keep things simple, there are basically four types of seeds you can buy:

1. GMO
2. Hybrid
3. Organic
4. Heirloom & open-pollinated

GMO SEEDS—You want to stay clear of all GMO seeds. GMO stands for Genetically Modified Organism. These seeds have genes that have been tampered with and changed in unnatural ways. They have been shown to potentially cause serious health issues. Avoid them at all costs.

Hybrid Seeds—There isn't anything bad for your health with hybrid seeds. The problem is that you can't save seeds from hybrid fruits. If you try, you can get plants, fruits and vegetables that look very different from the original. Furthermore, the seeds might not even sprout in the first place. There are so many other great varieties of fruits and vegetables that I can't see why someone would go for hybrids over a plant from which you can harvest good seeds.

"Organic" Seeds—They may be either hybrids, heirloom, or simply open pollinated. "Organic" simply means they have been certified by the U.S. government as meeting certain Organic requirements—which means they can't be GMO.

Heirloom & Open-Pollinated Seeds—These are the best seeds for the holistic gardener. You can save the seeds from these plants! Both open-pollinated and heirloom seeds can be saved for generations. When you replant, they'll grow and be like the parent plant. (Unless you have issues with cross pollination. Some new favorite varieties have been developed by accidental cross-pollination in home gardens).

Heirloom seeds are open-pollinated varieties that have been around for a long time. Even though it takes many years (50-100) to technically be "heirloom", often people call open-pollinated seeds heirloom that have been around for less time. (I tend to call *all* open-pollinated seeds heirloom. It's simpler.)

There are thousands, if not millions of heirloom varieties you can try. You'll never run out of options. My favorite heirloom seed company is Baker Creek.[1]

The reason to grow heirlooms is so you can save the seeds. Saving seeds from plants is a final gardening chore that has been going on for centuries, and it's not hard to do. True, it can be a very complicated subject, but it doesn't need to be. The only thing you need to worry about is keeping the varieties pure, and this varies for the different plants. Find a good book[2] and just start! Even if they aren't perfect, it's still better than nothing.

The Basics of Seed Saving

Seed saving can seem like a big deal, and to many people it is. When it comes to homesteading, most people aren't going to want to get overly involved in plant breeding. You don't need to do that to save seeds. Start with planting good seeds and begin saving the seeds they produce. You can save the seeds from the easy plants and keep buying the harder to harvest seeds too. Lettuce, beans and sunflowers are three of the easiest plants to save seeds from.

Lettuce—As the plant grows, harvest the outer leaves from the plant and leave the main part of the lettuce. When the weather gets hot it will bolt (meaning send up a stalk from the middle of the plant) and "go to seed". The stalk will flower and when the flowers die they will turn white. *(They look a lot like dandelion seeds.)* Under the white fuzz are the seeds. Pick them and let them completely dry in a brown paper bag. Sort and sift the seeds to separate off the seeds from the chaff. Store the seeds in a glass jar.

Sunflowers—When the flowers die, harvest the seeds by picking or rubbing them out of the flower head. (You may need to cover the seed heads as they ripen to keep the birds from eating them all. A brown paper sack can be placed over the heads and secured.)

Beans—Let fresh green beans ripen past the stage of snap beans into what we typically think of as dried beans. Then save the seeds like you would from a dried bean variety.

*** Make sure to always label and date all your seeds. Trust me. You'll forget what they are and their age if you don't.

Stories Behind the Seeds

There is fun history behind many heirloom seeds. Get a good catalog, and you can read about not only the shape, size and color of fruits and vegetables, but also how people used them in history. I once read about pepper seeds coming to America by a—I think Italian—lady sewing them up in the hem of her skirt. There's a variety of cowpeas that was a staple for the Southern armies during the 1860's. (Which most likely came over with the slaves when they came to America.) You can also find information about lots of the seeds Thomas Jefferson grew in his gardens, and what he thought about the different varieties. The list goes on! After learning these histories, you can buy and plant the same varieties right in your backyard.

The Garden & Your Homestead

The garden provides your family with high quality produce.

The garden is a place to teach yourself and then your kids (or younger siblings) diligence & hard work.

Vegetables can be grown and fed to your animals. Greens, grains, squash (winter & summer), beets, carrots, etc. are great to feed to your cows, goats, sheep, pigs, chickens, other fowl & rabbits.

The garden is often the starting point of a homestead.

You can grow carbon (straw, dead plants, etc.) to mulch your garden and/or for the compost.

After harvest, dead plants can be chopped up and fed to your goats or laid on the soil as mulch. (Chop them really small if you're mulching bacterial soil.) You can also use them as carbon to make compost.

The garden gives food to beneficial insects and honey bees.

The garden may provide a place where you can put your chickens to work. They can eat bugs and clean up. Goats can clean up your after-harvest mess.

Soli Deo Gloria! —Julia

From the book:
The Holistic Homestead
© Copyright 2017 Julia Hubler
--ReformStead.com

Chapter 9: Multi-Purpose Herbs

Herbs serve many purposes on the homestead. They're great for you, your garden, your animals and your home in so many ways. There's more than one reason to grow herbs around your homestead. Let's look at several ways herbs connect with your homestead.

Herbs As Family Remedies

Herbs are great natural remedies for your family. They're powerful and there's one to help with pretty much everything. Make sure you research and know what you're doing before you start because they need to be used with care.

Herbs for Livestock

You can use herbs as remedies for your animals too. My favorite is garlic. It's a powerful remedy that helps with almost everything.

Herbs for Pollinators

Herbs bring in pollinators like honey bees *(a bonus if you're raising your own)*, wasps, butterflies, lacewings, and many other beneficial flying bugs. So plant tons of them in your garden, orchard and everywhere! You can't have too many herbs or pollinators.

Herbs As Natural Pest Control

Herbs attract good bugs and the strong scents ward off many bad bugs. So plant herbs all throughout all your vegetables, shrubs, flowers and trees. Rabbits dislike rosemary and lavender. If you have issues with rabbits, try growing a "wall" of rosemary and lavender around your garden.

Herbs for Flavor

Homegrown herbs are nothing like store-bought. Fresh herbs have so much more flavor and smell. It's also nice to run outdoors and grab what you need when you need it. This is so convenient!

Herbs Are Easy to Grow

A few herbs may be challenging to start, but once going, they're hardy growers. Most of the ones that aren't perennials reseed and you don't need to plant them again. They're an important, low-input piece to your homestead.

Plant Herbs Everywhere!

Grow tons of them! Plant them everywhere and plant many kinds...in the garden, around the house, under your fruit trees.

Four Super Easy Herbs to Grow & Why

1. **Basil**—It's the easiest to grow from seed. Don't buy a potted plant. Basil is too easy to grow from seed to waste money on plants. Add your fresh basil to recipes. Home-grown basil is nothing like "fresh" store-bought basil. Home-grown is so much better!
2. **Rosemary**—I've started all my rosemary shrubs from transplants. They're very tricky to start from seed. Rosemary grows fast and turns into a large bush unless pruned. It's great to walk out the backdoor and add rosemary to recipes.
3. **Cilantro**—This is one of my favorite herbs! It's easy to grow from seed, and it reseeds well. After the first planting, you may never need to plant it again. When it goes to seeds it attracts tons of beneficial insects—especially ladybugs. There's never too much cilantro.
4. **Mint**—Peppermint, spearmint, chocolate mint—pick your favorite! Starting mint from transplants is easiest. All mints are hardy growers and some people consider them invasive—*warning*. Plant mint in a pot if you're concerned about it taking over. We love to go out the back door, pick a few sprigs of mint and make tea or just eat the leaves plain.

Blue-purple hyssop & white cilantro flowers.
(This and the first pic in this chapter—of the thyme—were taken in the Guild Example #3 drawing on page 54.)

One More Connection—Let Them Go to Seed!

Letting herbs go to seed attracts lots of bees, lacewings, ladybugs, wasps and other good bugs. When you do, many will reseed, which means you may not need to keep planting them every year. I haven't needed to plant cilantro since I first planted it.

They grow, we eat some, then they flower and attract many ladybug larvae, bees, wasps, and other pollinators. Next, the seeds come, dry, and fall on the soil. The seeds wait until the conditions are right and then sprout.

Chapter 10: Weeds—A Problem or Temporary Solution?

What are weeds? Weeds are the plants that grow where you don't want them, and they compete with the plants you *want* to grow.

A weed in your part of the country may be a valued herb in another location. Take dandelions for example. It's a weed in much of the country and valued where it isn't. I've seen dandelion seeds for sale in a seed catalog, so someone's buying them.

We don't have chickweed here. I've heard it's a great green to feed to your chickens, but others think of it as a weed. *It all has to do with your perspective.*

> **Know Your Weeds!**
> Research and learn about the weeds that grow in your yard. Learn which are edible, which ones mine up minerals, etc. Know what your weeds are and what they're good for.

The 'Good Side' of Weeds

There are several things weeds are good for. Instead of dismissing everything you didn't plant as a "weed", find out what it is and see if it's good for one of the following:

Some Weeds Are Edible—Some are great for your health. Dandelions are a good example. They're good for you, and yet, they're weeds. You can eat them or add them to your salads. *When you eat weeds, use caution!* Be sure to research and know what you're eating—some weeds are poisonous.

Some Weeds Mine Up Minerals—The dandelion is one kind of weed that does this. Its deep taproot brings potassium and minerals from deep in the soil up to the surface. The plants growing near-by will benefit from the minerals deep rooted plants make available.

Minerals Made Available by Legumes

"A broad mix of species belongs under and within the vicinity of fruit trees... Red clover has the nitrogen-fixing capability, being a legume, which ties in nicely to comfrey's need for high nitrogen...which in turn will be made available to fruit tree roots in the form of ammonium by the action of soil life. Legumes are noted as well for raising available phosphorus levels. The humble dandelion is especially adept at drawing potassium up... Are we tuning in to how a diverse understory contributes homegrown fertility to the orchard through organic matter cycled through the soil food web? Minerals are being mined and brought to the surface by this array of taprooted plants..." —*The Holistic Orchard*[1]

Flowering Weeds Attract Pollinators—Many weeds flower and attract beneficial insects. (At the same time, flowering comes right before the seeds! You may want to pull or cut them before they reseed and self-plant lots of weed seeds in your vegetable garden.)

Microbes Like Plant Roots—Microbes were designed to need plant roots to thrive, and they'd rather have weed roots than no roots. Also, weeds shade the microbes in the soil from harsh extremes like the sun, heat, cold, and rain. Remember—*the more diversity, the better.*

Many Weeds Are Edible for Goats—Make sure the weeds you feed are safe for goats. If you're milking, research to see if the weeds could change the taste of the milk. Dandelions are safe and don't change the taste of the milk, but make sure to check any

---

Why the Dandelion?

I keep mentioning the dandelion because:
1. I've read many good things about them.
2. Many people have them.
3. They're amazing for so many things!

---

others before you let your happy goats enjoy! They love weeds, and this may be a great help to cut their feed bill.

How to Use Weeds—*Strategically!*

Just because some weeds are good in the garden, doesn't mean you let them do whatever *they* want. I'm not advocating that. They'll take nutrients, water and space from your vegetables and not all are good for your garden. *(Dandelions are only one kind of "weed".)* Thorns and thistles are part of the curse for a reason.

If you let weeds grow as much as they'd like, you'll never grow anything else! It's your job to take dominion of your homestead, including the weeds. Weeds need to be left and kept strategically, according to your desires, not theirs.

- Let a controlled number of dandelions (or cousins of theirs) and other "good weeds" grow in your guilds. If they're tall weeds let them grow, then chop them down and feed them to your goats. You can also lay them on the soil around the tree as mulch.
- Legume "weeds" can also be used strategically in your guilds, orchard and garden. Figure out which legumes grow naturally in your area.
- If you take a gardening break, don't try to keep your garden weed-free. Mulch it, and let whatever weeds grow through the mulch, grow. When you go to plant again, cut the weeds down right above (or just below, if you want to prevent regrowth) the soil line. (If it's a really invasive weed, you may want to uproot it, but be careful! Try to disrupt as little of the soil as possible.) Then you're ready to plant.
- You can grow weeds on purpose to feed to your goats and chickens. Cut and carry them to your critters, or bring them to the weeds and let them harvest for you.

Weeding With Goats

A few years ago, we went to the store and bought four, 4-foot by 16-foot fence cattle panels. We connected them together making a moveable fenced area and put six of our young goats inside it. (Our larger milking goats wouldn't have stayed in it.)

It worked great! I moved them around after they ate the weeds in their pen—so they always had new weeds. After about a month they had eaten most all of the weeds. (I noticed it would've been nice to have a sheep in there too. The goats ate the weeds, but try as I might, I couldn't get them to eat much of the grass.)

Towards the end of that month, they figured out how to get out of the pen, and after that, all they cared about was escaping. They found they liked my newly planted fruit trees more than the weeds—which couldn't keep happening.

They were pretty much done eating the weeds, so it worked out great! If I was to do it again, I'd use electric fence.

Goats Eat Trees!
A few years ago, we had a few goats in a movable pen in our garden to eat the weeds, and they got out. There wasn't much in there besides the weeds and a few fruit trees. I was looking at the trees to see if they harmed them, and they all looked fine. Then I realized there was an empty spot next to a fig tree where a newly planted pomegranate had been...I haven't seen it since!

The Microbial Gardener's Weed Solution...
"When it comes to preventing weeds in the first instance, nothing beats mulches. The nitrogen, phosphate, and sulfur weeds need to germinate and grow are tied up by the biology at the interface of the mulch and the soil...in addition to facing no light and a physical barrier to their growth, they are given a poor supply of nutrients..." — *Teaming With Microbes*[2]

How to Control Weeds
The microbial conscious gardener prevents weeds with—*mulch!* The other natural option is to pull or cut them.

With mature weeds, you'll need to pull them. Afterwards, mulch where they were to keep many more from popping up. Mulch on the soil makes it harder for the weed seeds to germinate, which means fewer weeds.

It's not like you'll never have another weed, but there will be far less. The few that do pop up are easy to cut (except Bermuda, which is a pain). If you decide to pull them, they come up with much less effort, due to the soil being looser and softer from the mulch.

I show you how to mulch back in Chapter 5. Mulching for weed control is pretty much the same. One quick tip—if you see little weeds sprouting, put a few inches of mulch on top of them. That's usually all it takes.

How to Weed...Pull or Cut?—There are some weeds it might be better to pull.

You'll need to use your best judgment. (For example: if they're really invasive, it may be best to get the roots, so they don't come back. Bermuda grass is one that we always try to get as many roots as we can.)

If you can, it's best to cut them and leave the roots in place. If you do pull them, try to disrupt as little of the soil as possible.

How to Cut Weeds & Leave the Roots—If you decide to cut them, you have two

different ways you can do it.

1. You can cut the stalk right above the soil, and know they'll most likely grow back. (I love to do this with the dandelions in our fruit tree guilds. I want the dandelions there.)
2. The other option is to dig about an inch down, right around the stalk, until you see the white part of the root. Cut off an inch or so after the white part of the root starts. The roots will die and leave all their good substances to improve the soil. They shouldn't grow back.

In our annual vegetable garden, we pull weeds more often than in the orchard and guilds. It's easier, and we're all too often uprooting the noxious grass that grows around and through the weeds. Grass roots in the annual garden need to go no matter what!

How to Use Your Weeds

After weeding, there are four main ways you can turn the "wasted" weeds into a solution. Three of them we've already covered.

- Eat them.
- Feed them to your goats.
- Chop and drop them back on the soil as mulch.
- Compost them.

Bermuda Grass in the Garden is Another Story

Grass is the best when it's growing in the pasture. It's one of your **worst enemies** when growing in the garden. *(See page 53, for how to treat grass under your trees.)*

It's pretty discouraging when you get behind on grass. The best thing you can do (besides mulching and other things we've covered) is keep on top of it! Get as many of the roots as you can. Every piece of the roots remaining will grow back.

A Problem & a Temporary Solution!

There are times to weed, and there are times to let them grow. Sometimes weeds are your helpers, and other times they're your worst enemy.

Chapter 11: Beneficial Insects & Holistic Pest Control...

Besides being pretty, beneficial insects are *amazing* for your garden. Lots of beneficial insects flying around is a great sign of a healthy garden—even of healthy balanced microbes in the soil.

They all go together. A healthy population of good bugs is a sign that you have healthy plants, healthy soil, healthy microbes, and healthy vegetables to feed your family!

> ### Your Garden Allies...
> "Natural predators [beneficial insects] are too often judged as being insufficient at providing complete control of a pest problem...Dismissing helpful allies in the orchard ecosystem for not providing a complete solution on a species basis is exceedingly shortsighted." —*The Holistic Orchard*[1]

How Do You Get Beneficial Insects in Your Garden?

Grow lots of healthy plants that attract them. There are flowers they love more than others and it's good to know which they like. Try to plant ones that attract bees, ladybugs, lacewings, and wasps. At the end of this chapter I'll give you a sample list.

This is the best organic pest control. You want good bugs, so they can eat the bad bugs and keep your garden healthy.

Your garden allies! A ladybug is in the foreground and a ladybug larva is the black and orange bug behind it. Both eat insects. They're great for the holistic garden!

Some organic, homemade remedies can help with short-term problems. I'm not saying you shouldn't use them. Long-term, your solution is a healthy population of the good bugs.

Find a Healthy Balance

This *does* mean you'll have some bad bugs in your garden. That's okay. You need to have bad bugs so the good bugs have something to eat and make them want to stay in your garden. *Your problem isn't the bad bugs, it's an unbalanced ratio of bad bugs to good bugs.*

Healthy microbes in the soil are important for this. If the microbes in the soil are balanced and happy, the beneficial insects want to be in your garden. A healthy, balanced population of microscopic bugs attracts a healthy, balanced population of the larger, good bugs. **You don't need a pest-free garden. You need a balanced garden.**

"In most instances, insects get out of hand in your garden because something is wrong with the soil food web, which normally maintains a balance between pests and predators. But you are not going to have a totally pest-free garden even with the soil food web in place...

If your soil food web is healthy, this community will help plants overcome any insect pests. If there are a few bad guys, you need to realize that these help maintain the good-guy populations." —*Teaming With Microbes*[2]

It Takes Time—The first few years are the hardest. It's difficult to achieve a healthy balance. After a year or two improving the soil and diversifying the plants you grow, it gets easier. *Don't give up!* Keep adding new plants, grow healthy soil and use natural remedies when you need them.

Aim for healthy soil and diversity of plants and flowers. This is the most important thing you can do for holistic pest control.

We have lots of all kinds of beneficial insects around our garden and homestead—lady bugs, many different kinds of flies and bees (in addition to houseflies and honey bees), lacewings, and so many more!

Plants to Grow for Them

Here are a few plants I've found they love. This is a short list to get you started. They love almost any flowers and flowering herbs you can grow!

- Bees love: dandelions, sunflowers, squash blossoms, cilantro, borage, the flowers on radishes (after they go to seed)
- Butterflies love: chamomile, cilantro, and they're also attracted to moist soil
- Ladybugs love: dill, cilantro—anything with aphids
- Wasps love: sunflowers, cilantro, the flowers on radishes (after they go to seed), dill, cilantro

Butterflies love chamomile! Go out in the middle of the day when it's hot to find them.

————————

(The first picture in this chapter is a bee on a borage flower.)

Chapter 12: Rainwater & Greywater on the Homestead...

If a holistic homestead is your goal, you'll need to optimize your home and land for rainwater and greywater.

The *goal* is what we're aiming for. It's where we're headed. This chapter is not, "how to install a full-scale system." There are whole books on that. *(See Resources Chapter, page 192.)* We're going to see what using rainwater and greywater could look like on your homestead.

```
Make Sure It's Legal First...
Make sure what you plan to do is legal in your county and/or state before doing it. Some of the things
mentioned in this chapter may not be legal in every state. Know your what you're allowed to do in
your area before proceeding.
```

The Value of Rainwater on a Homestead

When you think of harvesting rainwater, what probably comes to mind is rain gutters and storage tanks. That's great for people who live where it rains a lot and have the money to set it all up. There are easier and cheaper ways to do it though.

You don't need money to catch rainwater—just a shovel. You can catch rainwater in earthworks. Take your shovel, move the dirt and use the dirt and plants to catch rainwater. It's a great, economical waste solution for the homestead.

Earthworks and rainwater collecting may seem like a big deal if you've never heard of them. It isn't. Like most things, you just need to learn. It's easy! Once you know the principles, jump in, and adjust later if you need to or if you do something wrong. You'll learn as you go, but you can change it. *It's just dirt!*

Less Water Wasted With Earthworks

When your plants are optimized for catching rainwater, there is another bonus. When you need water with the hose, more of the water absorbs into the soil and goes where the plants need it.

Rainwater Optimized Earthworks

The goal is to catch as much water as possible as it runs across your land during a rain storm. Yes, you "catch" the water. You won't be able to see the water like if it was in a tank. It's in the soil.

(If you see water above the soil for a long time, you have a problem. The water should infiltrate into the soil quickly when done correctly. You don't want to see puddles for long.)

Make a plan that takes into account how the water flows and where it goes on your land when it rains. Then dig out your earthworks.

Your earthworks can look like: berms, basins, gardens sunk in the ground, terraces with retaining walls on slopes, drains pointing to mulched infiltration basins, diversion swales, and more! **The goal is to get water to *stop* running *off* your land.** Make it collect around your trees, pasture, garden and infiltrate into the soil. This way the plants will get more water and grow better.

When you finish digging your earthworks, you'll have lots of water in big puddles after the first rain. After you plant trees, shrubs, herbs, etc., in the earthworks you've dug, it'll look different after it rains. The water will absorb more quickly into the soil.

You want this. Sitting water can attract mosquitoes and cause anaerobic soil. You want rainwater to absorb into the soil *as fast as possible.*

Greywater—A Resource on the Homestead

Greywater a waste?! If that's what you think now, think again. Greywater can be a great resource on the homestead. A connection made, and another piece in the puzzle. (Greywater is the cleaner waste water that comes from your house. Everything except the black water—toilet and sometimes kitchen sink—is considered greywater.)

Resourcefulness is key to a holistic homestead in the dry western states, especially when it comes to water. When you have water you can reuse, don't let it go to waste. Running your clothes washer to a fruit tree or landscape plants is a great way to start with greywater.

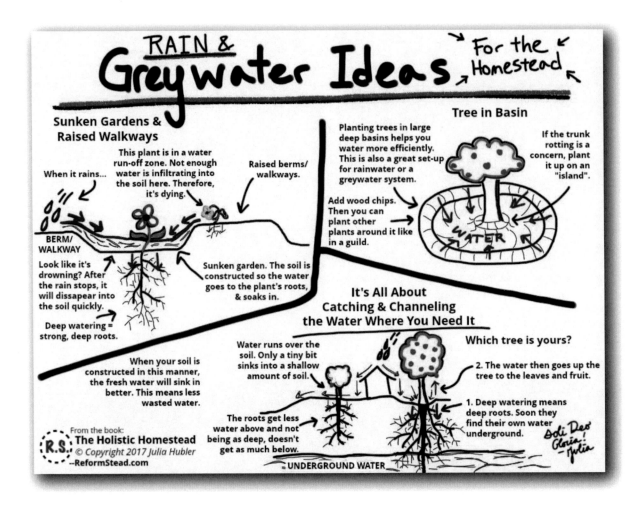

RAIN & Greywater Ideas *For the Homestead*

Sunken Gardens & Raised Walkways

When it rains...

This plant is in a water run-off zone. Not enough water is infiltrating into the soil here. Therefore, it's dying.

Raised berms/ walkways.

BERM/ WALKWAY

Look like it's drowning? After the rain stops, it will dissapear into the soil quickly.

Deep watering = strong, deep roots.

Sunken garden. The soil is constructed so the water goes to the plant's roots, & soaks in.

When your soil is constructed in this manner, the fresh water will sink in better. This means less wasted water.

Tree in Basin

Planting trees in large deep basins helps you water more efficiently. This is also a great set-up for rainwater or a greywater system.

If the trunk rotting is a concern, plant it up on an "island".

Add wood chips. Then you can plant other plants around it like in a guild.

WATER

It's All About Catching & Channeling the Water Where You Need It

Water runs over the soil. Only a tiny bit sinks into a shallow amount of soil.

The roots get less water above and not being as deep, doesn't get as much below.

Which tree is yours?

2. The water then goes up the tree to the leaves and fruit.

1. Deep watering means deep roots. Soon they find their own water underground.

Soli Deo Gloria! -Julia

UNDERGROUND WATER

A Few Simple Homestead-Friendly Greywater Ideas

When it comes to reusing greywater, there are simple systems and complex ones. Personally, I have no desire to try the complex greywater systems. They aren't any better than the simple systems, just different.

Greywater systems on your homestead can look like: running your clothes washing machine to a fruit tree guild, the hall bath sink and shower to a near-by blackberry patch, the kitchen sink to a mulched basin that waters a fruit tree, the R/O to flowers in the front, etc. There are so many options with greywater systems!

A simple greywater option is to have an outdoor sink that runs to a near-by tree. Get a sink and put it between the garden and the house to wash off vegetables before you take them in the kitchen. Have a hose attached to the drain that runs to a shade/fruit tree, or keep it even simpler. Have a drainage ditch that slopes down to a tree. When you wash the vegetables from the garden the water is being used again to water more produce. This can be an inexpensive set-up. Find an old used sink and then build a counter, stand, or something to hold it up.

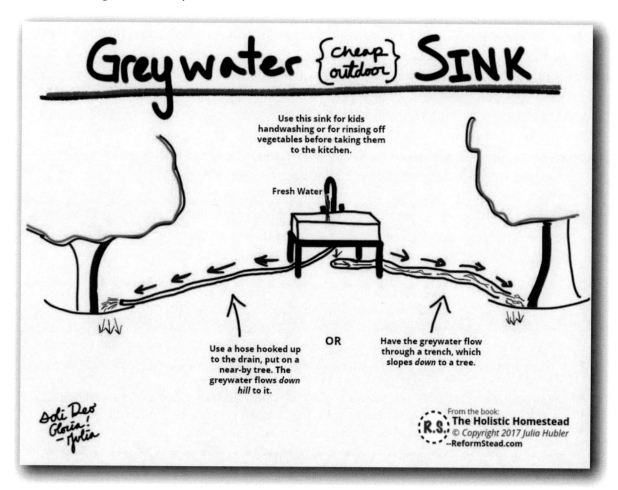

Health Issues & Greywater

"In practice, the health risk of greywater use has proven minimal to nonexistent...there has not been a single documented case of greywater-transmitted illness in the US." —*Create An Oasis With Greywater* [1]

How to Use Greywater—Clean & Safe

There are a few important rules you need to follow with greywater. Because of the risks, *don't* use greywater on annual vegetables, or any annuals you'll eat. Only use greywater on perennial fruits and landscape plants you won't eat.

When using greywater, you need the impurities filtered out. You need to cleanse your greywater by applying it to the soil correctly. It's easy!

Make the water go into mulch (wood chips are best) and continue down through the soil. When the water goes through the mulch and especially the top few inches of soil, there are thousands of microbes that will clean and purify the water—*more microbes again!*

Most of the cleansing microbes are in the top few inches of soil. As you go down a few feet, there are fewer microbes and the water isn't going to get as clean. The dirty water septic systems put underneath these important microbes miss an important cleaning. This uncleaned water is then infiltrating into your water table below.

For this reason, it's best to get as much water off the septic by setting up a greywater system on your homestead. This doesn't need to be done overnight. Start with the clothes washer and move on from there. Take it one step at a time.

> **The Amazing Purification System in Soil**
>
> "Topsoil is a purification engine many times more powerful than engineered treatment plants or even septic systems, which discharge wastewater into the subsoil, below most of the treatment capacity."
>
> "Apply wastewater as close to the surface as possible, without causing an unsanitary condition--The top of the soil has a purification capacity thousands of times greater than 3' down, because 90% of the life is within a foot of the surface." —*Create An Oasis With Greywater* [2]

Plants to Grow for Greywater

There are lots of options when it comes to plants you can grow for greywater use. Greywater can be used on your non-edible landscape and perennial fruit trees.

Here's a list of several to get you started: Banana, avocado, mango, citrus, fig, pomegranate, bamboo, blackberry, raspberry, elderberry, grape, apple, peach, pear, plum, apricot, etc.

Don't water with greywater: strawberries, lettuce, beets,

> The basic rule is to water only perennials (fruit trees are perfect) and non-edible landscape plants with greywater. **Never** use greywater to water annual vegetables or annual fruits!

any other edible annual vegetables, and/or lawns. (Unless you have a big expensive system, it's not practical to water grass safely. Greywater needs to absorb into the soil, not run over the surface. With the right set up, I think you might be able to do it in a pasture setting, but I'm not sure. The greywater books I've read don't talk about pasture, just lawns. It's something you might ask a greywater authority.)

Quick Tip: A *Free* Chicken Food Source

When you boil vegetables or potatoes, the water that's leftover contains small amounts of vegetables and minerals. Instead of tossing the water, feed it to your chickens. If you can't feed it to your chickens give it to your dogs or use it to water your garden. No need to throw it away! Another bonus, is by not putting extra water down the drain you'll help your septic system last longer.
Make sure you cool the water to room temperature before feeding it to your chickens, dogs or garden.

Rainwater *AND* Greywater

Rainwater and greywater relate to each other. If you set up your house with a greywater system, it's also good to have rainwater directed to the same location as the greywater. Greywater has small bits of salt and other small particles in it. Your plants will do better to have an occasional rinse from *clean* rainwater. (Very occasionally if you live in AZ *winking smiley face*.)

The systems you set up for rainwater and greywater are similar. You'll work with a lot of the same plumbing parts, dirt, and wood chips for both projects. (Fewer plumbing parts with rainwater, unless you catch and store it.)

Both have to do with water. Both use earthworks, digging and building with dirt. Both are great for a holistic, permaculture homestead.

Although they're different, they're important to have and to have working together. Think about how one or the other can work on your homestead and you'll make good connections. Think how both can work together on your homestead, and you'll make *great* connections!

Rainwater + Greywater & Your Homestead

Use rain & greywater to water fruit trees--or guilds.

Rainwater & Greywater are an amazing asset to the homestead.

Soil & land designed to receive rainwater means you'll use less fresh water. This saves money and water.

Your shade & fruit trees benefit from the water-filtration-friendly soil construction and the extra water.

A homestead optimized for rain & greywater is greener and more productive.

Rain

Grey

The fruit harvest from the trees is a great bonus!

Greywater is now a resource instead of liability.

When you harvest rain or greywater, more water is going into the soil--where it's suposed to be--which is good for the water table.

Soli Deo Gloria! -Julia

From the book:
The Holistic Homestead
© Copyright 2017 Julia Hubler
--ReformStead.com

Chapter 13: Holistic Chickens...

Chickens are a great animal to start with on a homestead. They are small and easy compared to other animals like cows, goats, or sheep. There's so much you can do with chickens. In this chapter we're going to look at chicken keeping from a holistic, permaculture (or call it a logical) perspective.

Anyone can keep chickens. I'm not here to discourage you. It takes more than 10 minutes online reading and a trip to the feed store to master your chicken raising skills. If you want to be successful at it, be prepared to put in a little time and work.

You may find it to be more of a challenge than friends make it out to be. It's always discouraging when hens aren't laying enough eggs, or they start eating them. Chickens are work, but they are totally worth it. Just don't think you're going to grab a few chickens, and come home with cute little peeps and automatically you're an instant pro. There's work and learning ahead. Be ready for it—you're going to have fun and learn a lot!

Remember, we're thinking holistically. The purpose of this chapter is not to give you a 'how-to' on the bare-bones of raising chickens. There are tons of books you can read and thousands of articles online for that purpose. *(See Resources Chapter, page 192.)*

Dual Purpose or Not?

When you buy chickens, you'll notice they tend to classify them in three categories—egg layers, meat birds (or broilers), and dual purpose.

Egg layers lay lots of eggs and don't have much meat on them. Meat birds are bred to pack on the meat—they don't lay many eggs. Dual purpose chickens, are bred to give both eggs and meat. They produce less meat than a broiler, and fewer eggs than a chicken bred to lay lots of eggs.

Many dual purpose breeds are the more old-fashioned heritage breeds. They are best if you want to breed chickens. Many of the other breeds are hybrids. (If you have hybrids, don't try hatching chicks. If you could get fertile eggs—which won't always work—their offspring can turn out very different from their parents. It's not worth your time and trouble.)

Dual purpose breeds are the more sustainable option. The dedicated egg layers or broilers have their place—it just depends on what you want. We have dual purpose hens for eggs and plan to raise broilers for meat. This set-up can be a temporary (or permanent) solution to buying chicken from the store—for both sustainability and health reasons.

How to Find & Buy Holistic Chickens

One reason to buy from a breeder (instead of a hatchery) is the genetics. If you're thinking "holistic," you'll want to breed your future chickens. The genetics in the birds you get from the hatcheries aren't good for this. Hatcheries don't selectively breed. They breed for quantity. Buy from a breeder who is selective in their breeding—one who cares and knows what they are doing. This is the optimal solution for the holistic homesteader.

Starting with quality stock can set you up for success in your backyard flock. Even better than finding just any good breeder is finding a good, local breeder. The best is if you can find a great breeder who is in driving distance. You can go meet the breeder and develop a relationship with him. Most will be friendly, glad to answer your questions, and give you advice from what they have learned.

One great thing about this is that the breeder's knowledge will be relevant to your climate. Many of the same conditions and problems you'll be facing, they have already been through. They will know what challenges you'll be up against and be able to help you out. Most breeders are glad to help.

Sadly, not everyone is going to have a good breeder nearby. In that case you can look online for the closest one. Once you find someone who looks good, you can discuss shipping. Most are willing ship their birds so you can still get quality breeding genetics. This is what we did when we bought our first batch of chickens from a breeder. I found a lady in California. We talked a lot through email and then as soon as she had some baby chicks available, she shipped them to me. Same as the hatcheries, only these birds had the better genetics. *(See the resources at the end, for a few websites to start your search for heritage breeds.)*[1]

I have presented better goals that the holistic homesteader wants to aim for. Don't let high standards stop you! If you do, you've misunderstood. Buying heritage chickens from a local breeder is an investment. It is worth it. If you can't afford it now, it's better to get started with cheaper chicks from your feed store or an online hatchery.

Go Beyond the Basics: Food & Water

Feeding chickens can be as easy as buying every crumb of their feed in a bag that has been pre-made "perfectly" for the chickens. Watering can be as easy as dumping some water in a dish for them. That's not where the holistic homesteader wants to stay. Feeding commercially produced feed is a great startup option. If that is your long-term plan, be prepared to pay an arm and a leg for it.

The Goal Is to Cut the Feed Bill

If that's not your goal—you've never owned chickens! Everyone who owns chickens knows they can cost a lot to feed. We're always looking for ways to cut back on feed costs. I have some good news...

It doesn't need to cost so much!

If you're willing to do a little extra work you can grow plants, herbs, bugs, compost and trees to provide food for your flock.

When you're considering how to cut your feed bill, I think the number one thing that comes to mind is this: you need to have *multiple sources* for the food you are providing them.

You can't expect to plant a fruit tree and not buy feed for your chickens anymore. You need to plan on multiple sources and have them all in line before you can decrease—and eventually cut—the store bought feed.

If you're already homesteading you may have more food sources for chickens than you realize. Let's talk about what chickens eat and how you can plan to get your chickens off so much store bought feed.

Chickens will eat just about anything—bugs, grass, greens, herbs, fruit, seeds, grain, meat (including chicken), milk, vegetables, bugs and larvae found in manure. You name it, they'll eat it.

Another thing to consider besides the variety of foods, is how many food sources you have in comparison to your number of chickens. You don't want to have so many chickens that there isn't enough food to go around. Depending on what your food sources are, how much they produce, etc.—there's a lot of room for variation. I can't give you a set number.

Also, realize some of your food sources are seasonal. There are seasons where there's more food available and times when it's scarce. For example, a mulberry tree will drop its fruit in the summer. The rest of the year it isn't producing food. It's giving lots of shade, though. This is a big reason for variety. Only one food source won't work. Have two and you're doing better. Notch it up to five or ten and you might have it! *The more variety, the more stability.*

Now that you've got an overview, let delve into the specifics.

Two Kinds of Live Feed for Your Chickens

There are so many options out there when it comes to growing live chicken feed. What do I mean by live feed? Bugs, worms, larvae, and insects are one kind of live chicken feed.

This is one area in which I've done more research than had first-hand experience. Outside of the compost and manure they have access to, my chickens have yet to taste a mealworm or bug I grew specifically for them.

There are many options online for building systems for raising mealworms, black soldier flies, maggots, and more. I like how especially easy the maggot buckets sound and how the maggot buckets help *lower the fly population* on the homestead. They're currently at the top of my to-do list. Most of the systems out there are pretty simple and straightforward and they offer great variety to your home-grown chicken feeds.

There are other ways to grow live feed, though. We let our chickens have access to the space around our larger animals (goats and a cow). The chickens pick through their manure and eat all the bugs, maggots and undigested food which passed through the animals. Not only is this a great chicken feed source, it's also great for the animals and land. The chickens going through are able to eat the bad bugs in the manure which can make the animal or the soil sick.

Teaching Chickens
When we got our cow I was glad we already had chickens. I've read how great chickens are at picking through manure and eating bugs. They did a great job with our goats! After a month of waiting for them, I realized—they didn't get it. They weren't going to figure this out. So I took their feed and sprinkled it on the cow patties. I did this a few times and that was all it took. They know what to do now.

Chickens in the Orchard

If you have an orchard, you can move your chickens in there once or twice a year to clean up the fallen fruit. Not only is this feeding the chickens, its keeping your orchard healthy by not letting bad bugs multiply in the rotten fruit. The chickens also fertilize your trees.

Growing Maggots for Chicken Feed & Fly Control

Yes, this may sound gross. Many people like this method as one more step to help cut their feed costs and flies in one shot. Here's one way to do it:

Get a wire basket and line it with straw. Hang or attach it in your coop in a way that the maggots will be able to fall out the bottom of the basket onto the ground after they hatch. Then place leftover meat bones on top of the straw and cover with a little more straw. Wait a few days and you should have little maggots dropping out of the bottom of the basket onto the ground and into your happy chickens' mouths.

If you're worrying about odors, it may smell a bit for the first few days, but after that it shouldn't. The straw also helps keep the odors down.

If you're thinking this might add to your fly problems, it actually works the *opposite* way. The chickens are eating the maggots that other wise would turn into flies. So, over time you are lowering the fly population on your homestead. It's natural fly control.

After there aren't so many maggots, take the straw and whatever is left and add it to your compost pile. Let it turn it into rich soil for your garden.

(I've also seen this online where people do the same thing, only in a five gallon bucket. They drill holes in the bottom, and the maggots fall out through the holes to the chickens. A bonus with the bucket is how easy it is to hang where you need it.)

Compost as Feed for Your Chickens & Garden—We talked about this in the earlier chapter on compost. Composting with chickens is great on the holistic homestead. It's an economical method for feeding both the chickens and garden.

It's possible to cut your whole chicken feed bill by composting. There are people who do it. The first one I heard about was a guy way up north who makes and sells compost on a large scale. He doesn't buy his chickens feed. He gives them free-range access to his compost piles. His system is great, and the eggs give him an additional monetary source to compliment his main income—compost.

We haven't done it to that extent. We do compost and the chickens have access to it. It's fun to watch them tear through the piles. They love eating and scratching in compost.

Let your chickens in the compost pile and they will tear it down. When they tear it down, they're saving you the trouble of doing it yourself. This means less work for you. When it comes time to "turn" the pile, all you need to do is put it back together. The chickens also help the compost by giving it manure—another bonus! Chickens and compost are a good match.

The Second Live Food—you can also grow greens and plants for your chickens. Plants like herbs, greens, vegetables, and fruits are important for a healthy chicken's diet. You can grow these for them right outside their coop, or you can cut and haul them from your garden to the chickens. *(See Chapter 8)* Sprouting grains is also an economical and healthy chicken food option.

Another live plant you can grow for them is grass. Chickens should always be on good pasture. (Make sure you provide enough room! Chicken manure can burn grass with the high amount of nitrogen it contains.) Grass is amazing for the chicken's health and the quality of the fats in the eggs and meat you get to eat from them. It provides more omega-3 fatty acids and *deep orange yolks!*

Quick Tip: The Clean Water Trick

Place a pallet under your chickens' water to keep it clean. A lot less dirt and rocks get in their water this way and the water stays much cleaner. Find a free pallet and put it to good use.

It's important to keep your chickens' water clean. Your chickens' health will suffer if you do not. This simple trick is my favorite way to keep their water cleaner all day.

You can also use this method for any other liquids you feed them. (Kefir, milk, broth, boiled vegetable water, etc.)

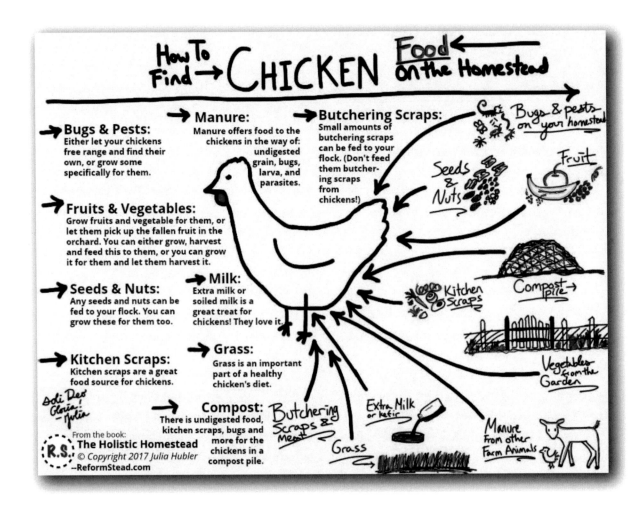

How To Find → CHICKEN Food ← on the Homestead

Bugs & Pests: Either let your chickens free range and find their own, or grow some specifically for them.

Manure: Manure offers food to the chickens in the way of: undigested grain, bugs, larva, and parasites.

Butchering Scraps: Small amounts of butchering scraps can be fed to your flock. (Don't feed them butchering scraps from chickens!)

Fruits & Vegetables: Grow fruits and vegetable for them, or let them pick up the fallen fruit in the orchard. You can either grow, harvest and feed this to them, or you can grow it for them and let them harvest it.

Seeds & Nuts: Any seeds and nuts can be fed to your flock. You can grow these for them too.

Milk: Extra milk or soiled milk is a great treat for chickens! They love it.

Kitchen Scraps: Kitchen scraps are a great food source for chickens.

Grass: Grass is an important part of a healthy chicken's diet.

Compost: There is undigested food, kitchen scraps, bugs and more for the chickens in a compost pile.

Soli Deo Gloria! —Julia

From the book:
The Holistic Homestead
© Copyright 2017 Julia Hubler
--ReformStead.com

Bugs & pests on your homestead
Seeds & Nuts
Fruit
Kitchen Scraps
Compost pile
Vegetables from the Garden
Butchering Scraps & Meat
Extra Milk or kefir
Grass
Manure from other Farm Animals

Holistic Chicken Coops

When you build your chicken coop there are pros and cons to every kind of coop you could design. The biggest question when it comes to a chicken coop is: are you going to make it *movable* or *stationary*? A movable coop needs to be moved on a regular basis. You'll need to keep up with a stationary coop by continually adding and removing bedding. There's no perfect, work-free chicken coop.

The Pros & Cons of a Stationary Coop

A stationary coop is one that's built to stay where you put it. Many times there's concrete involved to keep it secure—right where it is. Both stationary and movable coops can be large or small, depending on the number of chickens you have.

The Pros:
- You don't need to move it all the time.
- The bedding in a stationary coop should be composted and used in the garden, which is a good thing.

The Cons:
- You need to keep up on their bedding. (Take out the old stuff and add in new bedding often enough so it doesn't smell.)
- You need to have enough carbon (aka: wood chips, straw, hay, etc.) for their bedding so it never smells. Which means you'll constantly be adding more.

The Pros & Cons of a Movable Coop

A movable coop is one that is made so you can move it around your homestead. They usually have wheels that make it even easier to get it around. The one pictured below is our A-frame coop. It has four small wheels that make it movable.

The Pros:
- You can move it where you want.
- The movability means you can fertilize different parts of your yard when they need it.

The Cons:
- You need to move them often, which takes consistent time and effort.

If you're about to build your coop, take into consideration the points mentioned and pick the best kind for your homestead. It's up to you. We have both and I can see advantages and disadvantages to each. I lean more towards going with the movable coops. I like the flexibility that comes with them. We let our chickens in the movable coop free-range during the day. Both can be holistic and are great options.

How to Best Manage the Coop You Have

If you already have one or the other, you don't need to make another. You can make your coop work holistically with what you have.

If it's a stationary coop, think of the bedding in the coop as compost. It's no longer a bad thing. When it's done with it's job in the the coop, move it to the garden to improve the soil.

If it's a movable coop, you move their manure (fertilizer) around with more control. Simply by moving their coop, you can fertilize your pasture, and then you can take them over to your orchard to fertilize your trees and eat the pests. Then take them to the garden, etc, etc. Rotate them around your homestead.

Holistic Chickens

Chickens are great for the homestead. They can be a challenge at times, but that's okay. Push through the difficulties and learn new things.

Holistic Chickens
Homestead

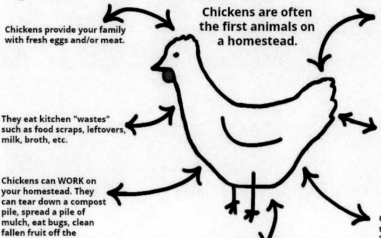

Chickens provide your family with fresh eggs and/or meat.

Chickens are often the first animals on a homestead.

Chickens add nitrogen to the compost, pasture, orchard and garden. (Wherever they go!)

They eat kitchen "wastes" such as food scraps, leftovers, milk, broth, etc.

They eat extra and overripe produce from the garden and orchard.

Chickens can WORK on your homestead. They can tear down a compost pile, spread a pile of mulch, eat bugs, clean fallen fruit off the orchard floor, etc.

Chickens are a great start for the homestead. They work even better in unison with other fowls: guineas, geese and ducks.

Chickens eat bugs, parasites, fly larva, scorpions, and more. They'll keep these away from your house, pastures, garden, and compost pile.

Soli Deo Gloria! —Julia

R.S. From the book:
The Holistic Homestead
© Copyright 2017 Julia Hubler
--ReformStead.com

Chapter 14: Beyond Chickens—Guineas, Ducks & More...

Chickens are a great start, but there are many benefits to having a *mixed* flock. Chickens, guineas, ducks and geese eat differently and provide slightly different benefits. There is some overlap, but you'll get more out of a diverse flock.

Guineas in the Garden & Homestead

One reason we bought guineas was to eat grasshoppers in the garden. We had a year where we had so many grasshoppers and they ate everything I planted as soon as it sprouted. I kept replanting and they kept eating it all. I even covered some of the seeds with sheets and they still got under them and ate the seedlings. Since we've had guineas roaming around, I've seen only a few grasshoppers, and we haven't had major trouble with them since.

The great thing with guineas is they don't tear up your garden. They don't dig around or eat the vegetation and fruits. They just mind their business and eat bugs. They're easy and amazing in the garden! You may need to protect new seedlings, but I'm not even sure that's necessary because they're so focused on the bugs. Chickens are another story.

Guineas like to be left alone. They won't let you get near them—they're scared of people. They will roam far and wide if you let them.

If your homestead runs out of bugs, they'll leave and go to where they can find more. Unless you keep them cooped up, you can't stop them from leaving because they fly much better than chickens. They don't fly a lot—they mostly stay on the ground like chickens. When they do fly, they can fly higher (maybe 10-20 feet) and further than a chicken can. (I've never heard of anyone clipping their wings. I don't think it would do any good.) Unless you have them penned up, you can't stop them. So far ours haven't left our perimeter fence. I guess the 16 we have find enough to eat on our two acres. (These numbers might help you gauge how many you want for your land.)

Guineas Eat Ants!—We were

having major issues with ants till we got guineas. The last 2-3 years with guineas, we've had far fewer ant problems. A puzzle piece in place—another great connection!

It's not like we never have ants, just not nearly as many of them. The ones we do have rarely cause trouble.

Guineas are great with a flock of chickens and the rest of your homestead because they're so easy. I don't feed them any special feed. Ours get in and share our chickens' feed, but they don't need it. They also clean up after the goats when they spill oats while I'm milking. When they're young chicks, they need feed starter and fresh greens. When they're full-grown you don't need to feed them. You can let them find their own food.

Warning! Many Fowls Are Loud

Guineas and geese make lots of noise—way more than chickens. While I like like the additional farm sounds, not everyone can have that much noise coming from their backyard. One nice thing about Muscovies is that they are supposed to be very quiet.

Ducks, Geese & Turkeys on the Homestead

We have chickens and guineas. That's why I've spent so much time on them. I've also read a lot about the other fowl. We'd like to get some if not all of these breeds in the future as well.

Ducks—Ducks make great egg layers. Many people like them because some duck breeds lay more eggs than their chickens. As with chickens, you have the breeds that are raised for either eggs or meat and the middle, dual purpose breeds.

They like to eat green forage (although they aren't as good grass eaters as geese), worms, insects, and are especially good at eating slugs and snails.

> **Permaculture—Ducks & Fruit Trees**
> While discussing the problems Japanese beetles can have on your fruit trees, Michael Phillips in, *The Holistic Orchard* says, "Then there's this permaculture nugget: You don't have a beetle problem, you have a duck deficiency." —*The Holistic Orchard* [1]

Geese—Geese are valued for their meat and only lay a few eggs. Their size makes them a great meat bird. Geese eat snails, slugs and are great grazers. They'll thrive on a grass only diet. As with other grazers on a multi-species homestead, geese like different kinds of grass, plants and seeds than chickens. A combination of fowl is the most efficient.

The presence of geese in the pasture may also help prevent attacks on chickens from aerial predators.

Muscovies—While often called ducks, they have a different wild ancestor and are more closely related to geese. They aren't true geese *or* ducks. They like to eat the same things your ducks and geese eat. They are excellent grazers and eat insects, worms, and slugs. They are prized as a meat breed and make good broody mothers.

Turkeys—These are another great fowl. Although I've heard of more problems associated with turkeys than other fowls, because they can be hard to get past the brooder stage. After that, they are supposed to be pretty hardy. Turkeys like to eat insects, grains and greens.

> **Diversify Your Flock**
> "I enjoy keeping a mixed poultry flock; species other than chickens can give us broader coverage of resource use and of other skills for work on the homestead or small farm." —*The Small-Scale Poultry Flock* [2]

Diversity Is the Key!

Seeing the varied types of food different fowl eat is helpful. Then you can see which would be best for you to start with and which may not be suited to your homestead.

Either way, a holistic homesteader's goal should be to have multiple species of fowl. The pros and cons of multiple breeds working together balance each other out, and you have a more *holistic* homestead.

FOWL on the Homestead

Chickens Eat:
Bugs
Parasites
Larvae
Food Scraps
Fruits
Vegetables
Manure

CHICKENS

Diversity in the home flock is most efficient for your homestead.

Guineas Eat:
Ants
Bugs
Bugs
& More Bugs

GUINEAS

TURKEYS

Ducks Eat:
Bugs
Worms
Snails
Slugs
Food Scraps
Fruits
Vegetables

DUCKS

Turkeys Eat:
Insects
Grains
Greens
Grass

GEESE

Geese Eat:
Snails
Slugs
Food Scraps
Fallen Fruit in the orchard
Vegetables
Pasure. Geese can thrive on
a pasture-based diet.

Soli Deo
Gloria!
—Julia

From the book:
R.S. **The Holistic Homestead**
© Copyright 2017 Julia Hubler
--ReformStead.com

Chapter 15: Milk Cows & Goats, Part 1: Which Is Best for You?

A milk goat or cow is often high on the homesteader's list. There are so many great things you can do with backyard-fresh raw milk!

How are you going to make your goat or cow fit holistically with the rest of your homestead? Is your land/yard better suited to a cow or a goat? Can a goat help keep down some weeds while giving you milk? Would a family milk cow be a better solution to improve your pasture and meet higher milk needs? *Do you have a preference?*

Let's get past the basics here and find the connections. How is your goat or cow going to best fit into your homestead? Let's see how to best add a milk animal to your homestead.

The Right Milker for Your Family—Goats vs. Cows

A few goats, a family milk cow—*or both?* Which is right for you? The answer to this question depends a lot on your goals and what you want. Let's compare the differences between goats and cows. Comparing can help you decide which animal is right (or wrong) for your family.

Goats vs. Cows: Size

Goats are smaller. This makes them easier to control and manage. They can be stubborn, but the fact that they're smaller makes them less intimidating and easier to handle when they get difficult.

Cows range more in size. An "old-fashioned" cow (more on old-fashioned cows in the next chapter) is smaller than the industry milk cows. Both are larger than a goat. That being said, they aren't known for being stubborn like goats. However, if you're new to working with animals, their size alone can be intimidating.

Size is also something to consider with younger children. You want to make sure to keep your little ones safe. A mean goat with horns could be more dangerous than a big, gentle cow—something to keep in mind.

Goats vs. Cows: Fencing

You need a fence that will keep your animals in. It doesn't need to be like Fort Knox, just contain the animals you have.

Goats and sheep are the hardest animals to control. Cows are easier. Here is a great rule of thumb is found in Joel Salatin's book, *You Can Farm*:

"Any fence that will keep in a sheep or goat will control cattle." [1]

You can set up a permanent fence, movable pens, or electric fence. They all have their pros and cons.

With permanent fencing, you set it up and there's little maintenance for many years to come. It stays where you put it though, and you can't change it easily.

Buy some cattle panels and connect them together and you can rotate small numbers of animals on your pasture. I know friends who use this for their sheep, and it works. I've tried it with goats and our cow. It works for a while, then they learn how to get out. That trick, once learned, is often repeated until you get a new fence, or reinforce it with t-posts. *(Not fun!)*

Electric fence is a popular, movable, affordable, easy fencing method among homesteaders right now. We're in the process of setting it up for our goats and cow. Electric fence is also a great fencing option for your other animals.

Goats vs. Cows: Feeding

It costs more to feed a cow than a goat for one simple reason: they eat more.

Feeding Goats—Hay is what most people start with. Feeding alfalfa hay is a great way to begin raising goats. This may be all you ever need or want to feed them.

Goats are great foragers. They like a varied diet with a little of everything. Grass is not their favorite, but they'll eat it if there's nothing else. They like things like weeds, trees and trimmings, and sticky things like branches and twigs. Part of their diet can be pasture, but they do best with a combination of things. 'Brushy' land would be great for goats.

We feed our goats a diet of alfalfa hay and supplement with as many weeds, trimmings, etc., when we can.

Make sure when you're feeding weeds and tree trimmings that they're safe for your goats. Do a quick internet search to see which plants that you have will make good goat food. (Milk flavor is another factor to consider with weeds too.)

Apple Trimmings for Your Goats...

I can't remember where I heard this—it's great on the holistic homestead. Goats love to eat apple tree branches and apple trees are good for goats to eat. So next time you trim your apple trees feed the trimmings to your goats. (Also, make sure your goats can't get to your growing apple trees.) You can feed trimmings from other trees as well, just make sure the trees aren't poisonous to goats before you feed them.

Weeds & Your Goats...

Weeds are great to feed your goats. (Be sure the weeds you feed them aren't poisonous first!) Dandelions and mallow are two weeds we have lots of here and they're great for the goats to eat. I let them grow tall and then chop them down and carry them to the goats. They love the occasional treat!

Feeding Cows—Again, many people who buy a cow feed her hay—even if it's just through the winter. Unlike goats, though, cows are great on pasture.

Cows are really easy to feed when they're on pasture. Provide adequate movable fencing and move them to new pasture every day or so. Give them some water and supplement with minerals and kelp. Then watch as she harvests her own meals.

Food Source for Animals on the Homestead

Carrots, winter squash, beets, pumpkins—and similar produce—can be grown and fed to your goats, cows, sheep, pigs and rabbits. This was a common practice many years ago. The fall harvest was stored and fed over the winter when there was no fresh grass.

"The best ones [pumpkins] were put in the cellar to make pumpkin pies, and the rest were piled on the South-Barn Floor. Every night Almanzo cut up some of them with a hatchet, and fed them to the cows and calves and oxen." —*Farmer Boy, by Laura Ingalls Wilder* [2]

Goats vs. Cows: Manure

Goat manure is small and there's less of it. It's also less messy than cow manure. This is great if you don't have a lot of space or don't have them on pasture. Less manure also means less compost for the garden and/or fertilizer for the pasture.

Cows' manure is different. It comes in messy piles, which are not fun to step in. This problem can be reduced with chickens. The other option with cow manure is to collect and compost it.

Goats vs. Cows: Milk Quantity

If your family is small, a goat would be perfect to give enough (but not too much) milk. It's hard to give an average. Goats range in milk production from less than a gallon up to 3 gallons a day. It's easy to multiply your milk supply to fit your family's needs by adding another goat or two. I've found three goats is great for our family of eight. On average, our three goats give us two gallons a day.

Cows give more milk, but it depends on the cow as to exactly how much. The modern commercial-bred cow can give over 10 gallons a day. The "old-fashioned" mini and small standard cows give 2-3 gallons a day.

Note: The numbers for both the goats and cows vary depending on the individual animal and how much grain you're feeding them.

Goats vs. Cows: Milk Flavor

I love the taste of our raw goat's milk. I don't see why everyone doesn't like it, but some people don't. Consider whether or not your family likes it. If you've never had it before, find some **fresh raw** goats milk and try it first. Don't get it from the store. It's not the same as fresh from a friend's backyard.

Cows' milk is the one everyone in the US is used to. (It's interesting to note though, in many other countries goats milk is more popular than cow milk.) Please note there is a difference in taste between store-bought and raw milk. Both raw goat's and raw cow's milk may take some getting used to if you're not accustomed to it.

Goats vs. Cows: Cream

The sad thing about goats milk is that it doesn't separate. All you'll get on the top of goats milk is a thin "film" of cream. If your family eats a lot of cream—or butter—you'll want to get a cow. Cows are known for giving lots of cream, which is great to make butter, sour cream, cream cheese and more!

Goat vs. Cows: Temperament

Goats have a reputation of being headstrong. They're small though, so it's not a big issue. I don't mind it—they're goats and I don't let them rule the world as they'd like to. You get more comfortable with them after a while. I like my goats.

Cows are known to be more sweet and easygoing. Note—with both goats and cows, this is a *general* rule. Every animal is going to be different.

Goats vs. Cows: Cost

Goats are more affordable than a cow. If you want healthy, fresh, raw milk and you want it fast, goats are a great, fast option. The cost is much less than a cow.

Cows are an investment. Especially if you're looking for a quality milk cow that's going to be productive for many years.

Deciding: A Goat or a Cow?

I'm glad we have both. I love our goat's milk, but we got our cow for the cream. Our goal is to have 2-3 milk goats and our milk Jersey. (This way we'll have milk when the cow is dry, and vice-versa.)

What do you want on your homestead? If you're on a smaller piece of land, goats may be great for you. If you have more land and a desire for rich creamy milk, a cow might be what you want. It depends on your situation.

There are a few other factors you may want to consider before you buy your goat or cow. In the next chapter we'll be going over a few more important considerations.

How Goats & Cows Relate to Your Homestead
→ ⇐

Milk Cow

Kitchen
The goats and cow provide the kitchen with milk (and sometimes meat). They also give you a use for fresh vegetable scraps like carrot tops and beet greens if you don't eat them.

A Mixture Of Ruminants
A mixture of ruminants is the best for your homestead. They eat different things, they eat them in different ways (grass), and the parasites are different. When you have diversity, you take full advantage of your land, and pasture.

Diversity is key!

Milk Goat

Garden & Orchard
Animals supply the garden and orchard with fertilizer (or compost). They also eat greens, weeds, twigs (for the goats), pumpkins, squash, beets and more that are extras or grown for them.

Grass
The animals fertilize and mow the grass, improving the pasture.

Chickens
Your goats and cow provide the chickens with manure which provides, bugs, parasites, larvae, and undigested food for the chickens to eat.

Compost
Goats and cows provide compost with lots of nitrogen--in the form of manure.

Soli Deo Gloria! Julia

R.S.

From the book:
The Holistic Homestead
© Copyright 2017 Julia Hubler
--ReformStead.com

Chapter 16: Milk Cows & Goats, Part 2: Two Important Considerations

We've covered the obvious differences between goats and cows. There are two more significant things you need to consider. This could change what animal you get, or who you buy her from.

The First Important Consideration—A1 & A2

You should know this before you get your cow or goat. What are A1 & A2? First off—I'm going to keep it simple.

The A1 & A2 genetics have to do with the beta-casein proteins found in milk. The difference between A2 beta-casein and A1 beta-casein is the structure of the amino acids. The A2 has a stronger bond of amino acids. A1 has a "weak link" which causes a break in the chain and digestion problems in people who consume it.

> "...this tiny difference in the protein structure can have a major effect when the protein is digested." —*Devil In The Milk, by Keith Woodford* [1]

The A2 gene is the "healthy" gene. Goats and all other mammals have this A2 gene.

> "The first of these [A1 & A2 genes] to be identified by scientists was called A1 beta-casein. A2 beta-casein got that name because it was the second of the A variants to be identified. It was only later that science was able to show that A2 beta-casein was the original one." —*Devil In The Milk, by Keith Woodford* [2]

Most of America's (and a few other country's) modern, commercially bred cows have the A1 gene. *All other mammals have A2/A2 milk—including humans.* Many lesser-known cow breeds also have the A2 gene.

All Goats Are A2/A2

The nice thing about goats is you don't need to be concerned with this. All goats are A2/A2. This is part of the reason some people who are allergic to cows' milk have no problems drinking goats' milk.

> **A1/A1 & A2/A2—Or A1 & A2**
> You can say it either way. A cow with the A1 gene (A1/A1), has the bad mutated (changed) beta-casein protein in her milk. The A2 cow (A2/A2) has the good beta-casein protein. A cow that is half-and-half (A1/A2) has half the good gene and half the bad.

Really, How Bad Is A1/A1?

The A1 gene *may* be a cause of many allergies and health problems Americans have. There is good evidence to support this possibility.

The mutated A1 gene causes inflammation in the body. This inflammation from A1 milk may be the cause of health problems such as:

- Heart problems
- Schizophrenia
- Type 1 diabetes
- Instant rashes on babies who are fed A1 milk. (When switched over to A2 goats milk, the issues clear up.)
- Autism

These are possibilities. There has been very little research done, but the research that has been done *strongly* suggests a direct link between A1 milk and health problems.

Learning More—There isn't a lot of information out there. This subject isn't being researched like it could be. The main book written is called *Devil In The Milk,* by Keith Woodford [3]. This is considered to be *the* book on A1 and A2. It's full of information and is written in a way that's easy to understand.

Also, Faith from Misty Morning Farm [4] *(in Virginia)* has written a little about A1 vs. A2 online. Their Milking School Introduction DVD has a great interview with Dr. Paul Dettloff on A1 & A2 with more details. *(MistyMorningFarmVA.com)*

Making the Best of Your Situation

If you already have a cow, do you know her genetics? Get her tested and see what her genetics are, and then do the best you can in your circumstances. If you can't swap her out right away—which I'd imagine most couldn't—make a long term plan on how to get an A2/A2. You might try breeding with an A2 bull in hopes of getting an A2 heifer someday.

You have more control if you know this before you get a cow. I'll warn you though, a mini A2/A2 costs a lot! When we were looking, a mini A2/A2 Jersey was going to cost $7,000-$10,000. We couldn't afford that. We bought a A1/A2 with the plan of breeding for the A2/A2 gene in one of her future heifers, and then we'll keep the younger A2/A2 as our main milker. We hope to have the A2/A2 milk in the future. In the meantime we'll still have milk that is better than store-bought.

The Second Important Consideration—Cows vs. Cows

Nope, that wasn't a typo. While we're hashing over goats vs. cows, you need to know that not all cows are the same. Most common today is the modern, commercially-bred dairy cow. There's also a cow with old-fashioned genetics. In this book I call her the old-fashioned family milk cow. It's the genetics that make the difference. Depending on your situation, the cow you get may make or break your experience.[5]

High Concentrates vs. Grazing Genetics

Commercial dairies want as much milk as possible, and they sacrifice a great deal for it. This is a sacrifice most family homesteaders can't afford. Concentrates like grains are expensive to buy and/or produce. Commercial dairies can afford it, but it's hard on a small homestead.

By "high concentrates," I mean a lot of grain is being fed to the cows. They may feed other concentrates, but grain is the big one.

God made cows to eat grass. There's nothing wrong with feeding your cow a little bit of grains every now and then, but in the wild, cows would probably come across them and eat what they found—which wouldn't have been much. When grain becomes the *foundation* of the cow's diet, that's when you have problems. It affects the cow and her calves. The cow's body now feels a *need* for large amounts of concentrates, and her offspring are bred to continue and reinforce those traits. You get more milk out of the cow, but the cow suffers for it. You get more milk for a few years, but then they start having problems.

Grazing genetics are old-fashioned genetics that cows had back before the small family milk cows were bred into commercial dairy cows (150+ years ago). Old-fashioned cows with grazing genetics have the ability to thrive on grass and pasture with a tiny bit to no grains. They're the kind of cows families owned and raised on their homesteads for hundreds of years, without all the problems and issues many families, homesteaders and commercial dairies have today.

A Cow That Wouldn't Eat Grass Started My Research

I was talking to a friend one time and she told me her cow didn't eat their grass, and they had to buy all her alfalfa hay. I was shocked! Who ever heard of a cow not eating grass?

This lead me to start researching. It was a lot of work! For the longest time I couldn't find anyone anywhere who talked about cows not eating grass. Even more important, how to fix the problem!

I was thinking, trying to figure it out, and doing lots of research. I decided it must be our "new" cows bred for the commercial dairies. Think about it. The cows most families owned over a hundred years ago ate grass. They didn't feed their cows bucket loads of grain every day, but I had no proof. I needed to find evidence.

After lots of researching, I found Misty Morning Farm's website. They talked about grazing genetics, the exact thing I was looking for but I didn't know it even had a name! I also learned you should leave the calf to nurse on his mom 4x longer than the commercial dairies—for proper rumen development. This also helps them digest their food better and live longer.

I soon read everything on their site. They knew what they were talking about, and finally it all made sense.

Tons of Milk vs. A Moderate Amount

Two to three gallons of milk a day for a family is reasonable—ten isn't. You'd better plan on selling a lot of milk if you're going to get a high producing cow. I like the lower

115

number of gallons with the mid-mini cows. It's not too overwhelming and it's not too little (a mini gives less than a mid-mini). A mid-mini seemed like the best middle-ground route for our family.

Grains or No Grains?

When it comes to feeding grains you must remember what kind of genetics the cow has. Cows and goats are ruminants. They need a diet of mostly grass—or weeds. When you feed grain, it can upset their stomachs and rumen. Feeding too many grains long-term can lead to health problems or even the death of a cow.

Hearing this might make you want to go the opposite way and feed no grains. It's not that simple. You can cut back and try to wean your cow off of grains as much as possible, but you need to understand the *genetics* of the cow you're dealing with.

If she's a typical, commercially bred dairy cow, you may not be able to get her off of grain. She's been *bred* to live on a high grain diet. You can cause her problems if you cut it back drastically. She might lose a considerable amount of weight or come close to not producing any milk. Both problems defeat the purpose of owning a cow.

If you have one of these cows, make sure you watch their body weight and condition closely. When you start cutting back on her grain, do it slowly and pay close attention to her health.

If you get a cow with older genetics, one who for generations has been raised to thrive on grass, she'll do great with much less grain than is "normal"—or even none. I'm not opposed to feeding a cow some grain. It just needs to be in moderation. When I say moderation, I mean about a cup or two a day. (Not the huge amounts fed by commercial dairies (many pounds), or even the "tiny" few pounds by many homesteaders.) You need to know your cow, and what she can take. *Watch her closely if you're making changes in her diet.*

Don't Get a Soybean-Fed Cow!

"I have followed for many years the sickening effect of soy on ruminants. Cows that formerly could easily reach the age of 15 years and have 12 calves, have on average now less than three calves and reach hardly the age of 6. One main reason is the high percentage of soy in the rations. It works into the buildup of ammonia in the rumen. This affects negatively the liver and then shows up in mastitis and sterility. Off they go to the butcher. Only there can a vet identify the defective livers. The soybean, bringing about high milk yields in the first two lactations--is the curse of our cattle herds. And the milk achieved through it is not health promoting either...Trauger Groh PPNF Health Journal."
—Found in: *Nourishing Traditions, by Sally Fallon* [6]

Note: A calf whose dam or sire (mom or dad) was raised on soybeans may also be more susceptible to liver problems.

116
© Copyright 2017 | Julia Hubler | Soli Deo Gloria! *(Glory Be To God Alone!)*

Short Life vs. Long Life

A commercially bred cow living on your homestead with proper care and cleanliness is most often going to have a longer life than the cows in commercial dairy farms. They're packed in huge, filthy, and chemical-laden pens with fecal matter for their bed.

I was shocked to learn how short a typical dairy cow's life was. When you think about it, it makes sense. Dairy farms aren't the place to go for your health—or sense of smell. Consider the cows living in that odor and muck 24-7.

A quality, old-fashioned milk cow is different. As long as everything goes right, she'll live and be productive well into her teen years.

> ### The Life Span of a Typical Dairy Cow
>
> "I was amazed to learn the…average number of lactations that the dairies get out of their cows is 1 1/2 to 3 at the most. I really did not believe it until I talked to the fourth vet." —*Misty Morning Farm* [7]
>
> "Dairy cows may continue to be economically productive for many lactation cycles. In theory a longevity of 10 lactations is possible. The chances of problems arising which may lead to a cow being culled are high, however; the average herd life of US Holstein is today fewer than 3 lactations. This requires more herd replacements to be reared or purchased. Over 90% of all cows are slaughtered for 4 main reasons: Infertility…Mastitis…Lameness…Production" — *Wikipedia* [8]

Big Cow vs. Small Cow

I found this interesting. The average size cow before the monopolized dairy breeding took over was what we now think of as "mid-mini" cows.

A hundred plus years ago before "the bigger the better" breeding practices came into play, she wasn't the size of a standard, and she wasn't the size of a mini. Industry bred them up for production, and the mini folks bred them down.

Short Time on Formula vs. Proper Time on Mama's Milk

A calf with inadequate time on her dam's milk will leave the calf with an underdeveloped rumen. Her rumen will never be able to make up for the loss. This can lead to health problems and a shorter life. Think about it. The rumen is the first stomach where they begin digesting their food. If the calf's body isn't able to properly digest the food she's eating, it isn't helping her like it should.

Modern dairy calves on average are on milk for 5-8 weeks. **One *quarter*** of what's needed for their rumens to develop. Four to six months—*not weeks*—is the time a calf needs to be on her dam's milk to ensure correct rumen development for a long, productive life.

In addition, dairies typically feed calves formula instead of their mama's milk. This too isn't as good for them.

Cheap vs. Quality

You get what you pay for. There are many more commercially bred cows on the market. They're also cheaper and easier to find. Just make sure you know what you're getting into before you buy one—count the cost. I'm not saying you can't make it work on your homestead, but to me, after researching it, they sound like way more work than they're worth.

If you can, save money to get an old-fashioned cow. In the long run she'll be better suited to your family. This may mean getting used to goats milk for a few years while you save. Most people can afford a good cow if they prioritize, plan, and save accordingly. Maybe in the future, families will start to request them more and the supply will go up and make them cheaper. We'll see.

The Commercial Dairy Cow vs. The Family Milk Cow

Modern Commercial Dairy Cow	"Old-Fashioned" Family Milk Cow
Bred to need high concentrates like grains. These cows no longer do well on a grass-only diet.	The "old-fashioned" cows with grazing genetics, like all cows had years ago, thrive on grass and pasture with only a tiny bit or no grains.
Modern cows are bred to give their owner as much milk as possible. (An average of 6-10 gallons a day)	These cows produce a family-friendly amount of milk. (About 2-3 gallons a day)
The average life span of a modern dairy cow is 1.5-3 lactations. (Or about 2.5-4 years.)	The average lifespan and productive milking years of a well-bred milk cow is into their teen years.
Because they're bred to produce as much milk as possible, these cows are huge! The average milk cow weighs up to 1,500 pounds.	Old-fashioned cows are smaller and more manageable. They average 500-800 pounds. The mid-mini isn't a new, smaller cow—they're the size of an old-fashioned cow. They're less common due to commercial breeding.
The typical age a commercial dairy calf is weaned is at 5-8 weeks. Even then, they're fed formula instead of their mother's milk. Having them on milk for this short time means their rumen doesn't have time to fully develop. An underdeveloped rumen is part of the reason for their health problems and short lifespan.	A good breeder lets their calves nurse instead of giving formula. They'll also let them nurse long enough. Calves should nurse for 4-6 months. This gives the calf's rumen enough time to fully mature and encourages a long, happy, and productive life.
Due to their availability, these cost less to get started with, but consider well the long-term costs.	There aren't many people raising them so they cost more. They're an investment—an amazing asset to your family for years to come.

How to Find an Old-Fashioned Family Milk Cow

Finding a local breeder may not be easy. I know of *one* farm that meets all of the above requirements. They're 2,000 miles away from us! Let's first narrow in on what you want in your family milk cow.

Requirements for a Family Milk Cow—You can take or leave what you like of this list. These are simply suggestions. A good milk cow must:

- Have generations of grazing genetics in her blood lines
- Be fed little to no grain
- Be raised on real milk for 4-6 months minimum
- Be small in size—a mini, mid-mini or small standard
- Come from a breeder who will assume she'll live and be producing into her teens
- Come from a farm that has been tested and proven to be free of diseases like; Johnes, BVD, TB and brucellosis

Where to Buy an Old-Fashioned Cow—It may be hard to find a good breeder—especially one near you. Look on Craigslist, do several google searches and see what you find.

The best breeder I found is located in the Shenandoah Valley of Virginia. On Misty Morning Farm's website[9] I was able to find a lot of extremely helpful information. I found more on their website than all the others I spent hours looking through put together. It's not like there aren't other good breeders out there—I'm sure there are. Misty Morning Farm is the only one I found educating folks online.

We bought a mid-mini Jersey from them in October 2016. I'm looking forward to learning more with our new cow. I've dreamed of having a milk cow for years, and I can't wait for all the butter, ice cream, cream cheese and more I'll get to make with her cream soon.

> **Cows As a Part of America's History**
>
> In 1624, the first cows arrived in the Plymouth Colony. In the early colonial days and up into the 1850's, most households in America owned a family milk cow. Then farmers gradually took it over and the family milk cow vanished from the vast majority of American lives.

Enjoying all the fresh milk and cream right from your back yard is a huge benefit to your family. You get to—as with the rest of the food you are raising—know exactly what is going into your food.

Making the Most of Your Resources

You may not be able to get a cow or goat with the exact traits you desire. That's okay. *Do the best with what you have* and the resources you're able to take advantage of. **Fresh, raw milk from any cow—or goat—is way healthier than anything you can buy from the store** and you know what's in it!

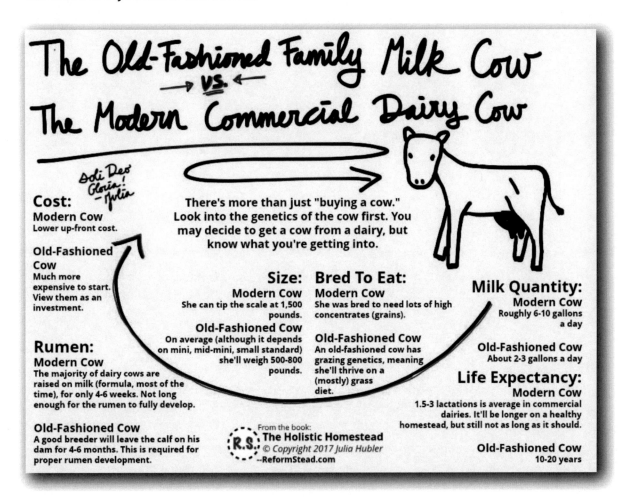

The Old-Fashioned Family Milk Cow
→ VS. ←
The Modern Commercial Dairy Cow

Soli Deo Gloria! —Julia

Cost:
Modern Cow
Lower up-front cost.

Old-Fashioned Cow
Much more expensive to start. View them as an investment.

There's more than just "buying a cow." Look into the genetics of the cow first. You may decide to get a cow from a dairy, but know what you're getting into.

Size:
Modern Cow
She can tip the scale at 1,500 pounds.
Old-Fashioned Cow
On average (although it depends on mini, mid-mini, small standard) she'll weigh 500-800 pounds.

Bred To Eat:
Modern Cow
She was bred to need lots of high concentrates (grains).
Old-Fashioned Cow
An old-fashioned cow has grazing genetics, meaning she'll thrive on a (mostly) grass diet.

Milk Quantity:
Modern Cow
Roughly 6-10 gallons a day
Old-Fashioned Cow
About 2-3 gallons a day

Rumen:
Modern Cow
The majority of dairy cows are raised on milk (formula, most of the time), for only 4-6 weeks. Not long enough for the rumen to fully develop.

Old-Fashioned Cow
A good breeder will leave the calf on his dam for 4-6 months. This is required for proper rumen development.

Life Expectancy:
Modern Cow
1.5-3 lactations is average in commercial dairies. It'll be longer on a healthy homestead, but still not as long as it should.

Old-Fashioned Cow
10-20 years

From the book:
R.S. **The Holistic Homestead**
© Copyright 2017 Julia Hubler
--ReformStead.com

Chapter 17: Milking Sanitation...

Everyone draws the line in a different place, and each person has their own opinion of what is "clean." One says, "Raw milk is amazing for you! Pasteurized milk is evil!" The other, "Raw milk will kill you! You have to pasteurize it!" Some individuals seem ready to fight World War 3 over it.

Who and what are you going to believe? Who's right? In one sense, there's truth to both sides. You need to ask an important question—*"What are the living and milking conditions like?"*

Keeping the Milk Clean Is KEY!

An ounce of prevention is worth pounds of cure. Instead of fixing problems you make for yourself, how about not making those difficulties to clean up? Isn't that easier?

It's best to keep the milk clean while you're milking. It's hard to go back and make dirty milk clean again.

Think About...

...the disgusting fecal matter & unsanitary conditions modern dairy cows are raised in, and think of how many chemicals and antibiotics are needed simply to keep the cow in "good health." How many chemicals are needed to make the milk *ahem* "fit for human consumption"?!

Eight Tips to Keep Milk Clean While You're Milking

1. Start by milking in a *clean* place. Clean off the milking stand or floor. If you're milking on the floor in a shed/barn, keep fresh pine shavings and straw down.

2. Only put your milk bucket down in a *clean* place. If you can, make a way to hang the bucket by the handle. Then you don't need to worry about finding a clean surface for it.

3. Keep your milk bucket covered. Use a lid or a piece of plastic wrap. Take the bucket out covered, uncover to milk, and then cover it right back up again.

4. If you're worried about hair falling in, brush her off before milking.

5. Keep the flies away while you're milking and your goat or cow will have one less reason to step in the milk bucket.

6. Take it into the house, strain it, and get it in the fridge and chilled, *as quickly as possible!*

7. After the milk is cooling, wash your milking supplies right away. They'll be clean and ready for the next milking.

8. If manure gets in your milk or it's dirty, consider it a good excuse to give the chickens and dogs a treat.

Commercial Dairies Are Different

It's no longer about one or two family cows out in the pasture and milked in a clean environment. Now you're talking about hundreds of cows in tight spaces. Manure covers the ground, cows, and even fills the air! It's asking for diseases and harmful microbes to take over.

Strong chemicals like bleach, processes like pasteurization, even antibiotics to keep the cows alive in such conditions, are, I believe, *needed* in the filthy modern commercial dairy farms I've seen. In all likelihood we'd end up with a sick America if they stopped their harsh cleanings and pasteurization. They'd have to make major changes in their raising, housing, feeding, and milking of the cows.

You're not in the same situation as they are! You're dealing with different circumstances—your homestead is clean and natural. Sure, you'll have times when things get out of hand, but it's not the same. Home-grown raw milk is much safer than if a commercial dairy were to sell raw milk.

Pasteurization & Bleach—or Not?

People have been drinking raw, unpasturized milk for thousands of years. Often it has been fermented in some way before consuming, nevertheless it's been raw. Most homesteaders aren't going to pasteurize the majority of their milk. Besides killing off all the good bacteria and enzymes that aid in digestion, it is also extra work.

I'm skeptical that bleach is as great as many people think it is. Either way, it is a harmful chemical we don't want on our homestead. (It can cause many different health problems.) We never use bleach on our milking equipment. We take other precautions and instead use cleaners that aren't harmful. Just because you don't use bleach doesn't mean you are not careful. Have *purpose* in your milk sanitation efforts.

- Wash milk bucket and strainer right away
- Use plain soap and water
- Every now and then give the bucket and strainer a deep cleaning in vinegar

The Natural Alternative to Bleach

Cheap white vinegar is a great homesteader's answer. Whenever my milking bucket needs a "better than soap" cleaning, I pull out the vinegar. Vinegar kills off a range of bacteria, mold and viruses. It's a great natural bleach replacement.

My Daily Milk Pail Cleaning "Recipe"

In many ways, cleaning starts all the way back when you're milking. Keep the milk inside the pail clean, but also keep the outside and bottom of the milk pail unsoiled. This gives you less cleaning at the sink.

The second important step to cleaning the bucket is to wash it *right away.* After the milk is chilling in the fridge, clean the milk bucket—*immediately.* This makes

124

the dirt and milk wash off faster and more efficiently. Letting it sit gives time for germs and bad bacteria to grow.

Those two are the most important steps to a clean milk pail. Now for the actual cleaning.

Ingredients: a bit of soap and **hot** water

1. While you wash, use the hottest water possible.
2. Rinse and scrub off the whole milk bucket with just water. Scrub until it looks clean, and there's no milk left. (Doing this means you won't dilute the soap with milk.)
3. Add a good size squirt of soap. Scrub it again—covering the whole bucket.
4. Rinse all the soap off and let it dry.

My Occasional Deep-Cleaning Recipe

Occasionally I'll deep clean my milk bucket. It's good to do if you don't wash it right away, or you can make it a once a week or month chore.

Ingredients: 2 cups of vinegar

- Fill up the sink with water and add in *about* 2 cups of vinegar. Cheap white vinegar works great.
- Soak it for 1-2 hours. If you don't have time, you can do it for less.
- After soaking, wash with soap and **hot** water.

Another way I know of people cleaning their milk bucket is to wash it in the dishwasher. If you have one, I'm sure it works well. *Our dishwasher is one of my younger siblings. *winking smiley face**

Air or Towel Dry?
I've read it is best to let your milk pail air-dry, due to bacteria that may be on the drying towel. I usually let our bucket air dry. Personally, I don't think it's a huge deal—as long as you use a fresh clean towel.

Kids Can Milk Too!

Children can be taught to milk as well. I taught my ten-year-old brother how to milk. It takes them some getting used to—which isn't fun. It's fun until after a few minutes when the hands start hurting, and then they don't want to do it anymore. Make them stick with it and soon they'll be as proficient at it as anyone! Children can also be taught milk sanitation rules. *(Although the younger they are the more supervision they'll need to be sure your family is drinking clean milk.)*

Chapter 18: Keeping Roosters, Bucks, Rams & Bulls

Keeping male animals is something every holistic homesteader needs to consider. You need to know your options and have an idea of what you're going to do—you need to make a plan.

You have three main options:

1. Keep the males
2. Borrow one from a neighbor
3. Artificial insemination (AI)

Keep Them

There are several valid reasons folks don't want to own and care for the males, but doing so makes it much easier when you need to breed.

Roosters

First, you only need roosters if you want to hatch chicks. The hens will lay eggs either way.

Housing & Fencing—They require the same accommodations as the hens. Nothing extra is required. In my opinion, they're easier to keep in a fence than a hen. Hens are more aggressive about escaping—at least in our experience.

Cost & Feeding—They don't add to your purchasing cost much. They can actually decrease your costs if you buy your chickens straight-run (meaning the seller ships whatever hatches without sexing them first).

Feeding them is where the extra costs come in, and they don't cost much to feed if you only have a few of them.

Temperament—While some roosters are mean and may hurt little children badly, not all breeds do. If you want roosters, get tame breeds—breeds meant to work well with a family. You can still get a mean rooster among the tame breeds, but it occurs less often. If that happens, cull him and turn him into roast chicken (or chickens stew if he's older).

Here are a few breeds known for having tame roosters:
- Australorps
- Buff Orpingtons
- Barred Plymouth Rock

Pros
- Having roosters gives you the option of hatching your hens' eggs.
- Roosters protect the hens from (some) predators.
- They keep the pecking order straight.
- They're beautiful!

Bucks *(Male Goats)*
If you keep a buck, he'll need separate fencing and housing from your other goats. Bucks smell bad and if you keep them with the does, your milk will have an extra goaty (bad) taste—something you probably don't want. (If you're raising meat goats, this isn't an issue and you can keep them together.)

As far as how hard they are to fence, the bucks we've dealt with have been pretty laid-back. We haven't had any trouble with them escaping.

Bucks are very easygoing and mellow. We've never had any trouble with them hurting anyone.

Just so you know: We've so far owned roosters and a buck, but not a ram or bull. The info here is from friends who have owned them, and things I've read.

Rams *(Male Sheep)*

There are two ways you can view this issue. You can keep them together with the rest of the flock all the time, or keep them separate and put them with the females at breeding time (like you would with the goats). There's no extra fencing costs when they're together, but there are some cons to this.

You never know when the ewes will lamb, so you could have babies anytime with no warning. The other is, after they lamb, you may want to separate the ram from the ewe and her lambs. The ram can cause problems with the lambs, and the ewes are defensive of their babies.

Unlike the bucks who are laid back, rams can be aggressive. They may try to knock you over if you turn your back on them.[1]

Bulls *(Male Cattle)*

Goat bucks need to be separate from the does because keeping them together can make the milk have an extra "goaty" taste. Bulls do not have this problem. A bull with your cow won't give the milk an off taste.

However, it is best **not** to keep a bull with your cow. The bulls can be mean to people and it's best not to bond with them. Leave them alone! Even a 600 pound mini Jersey could do some major damage, so keep children away from them! They may seem sweet and friendly, but it's not worth the risk. They could harm people or your children at any moment—with no warning.

Misty Morning Farm calls these their "Bull Rules:"
1. Keep the bull in a separate paddock.
2. Don't bond with your bull.
3. Keep children away from him at all times.
4. Leave him alone!

For this reason, separate fencing is required. You and your family want to bond with your cow, but not the bull. Fence him off in a separate paddock and bring him to your cow, or your cow to him, when you want her bred, and then separate them again.

Electric fencing is best for bulls. You'll need 2-3 strands of electric to keep a bull contained. Electric fencing is also best for cows. More than keeping *in* your cow, it also keeps the neighbor's bull *out*. (For extra protection, add a strand of electric about chest height on the outside of your fence.) [2]

Cost & Feeding Bucks, Rams & Bulls

You'll have the expense of buying them. This can be a little or a lot depending on how important the genetics are to you. If you just want to keep a goat producing milk, that's not as much as wanting to breed and sell high-quality calves from your milk cow.

Feeding them is where the costs are going to get you. Unless you have land and pasture to spare, a bull is going to eat a lot. Rams and bucks will eat less, but it'll still add up.

The Pros of Owning a Buck, Ram and/or Bull

It's by far the easiest when you need to breed! You save yourself time, money and a headache.

Borrow One

A neighbor who has a male that you can borrow or pay stud fees to may be best. It may be easier than dealing with all that goes into keeping one on your homestead.

If you don't have a neighbor in walking distance, you may have trouble getting a male when you need him. This depends on where you live and if you have a way of transporting either the male to your homestead or your female to their place.

The cost isn't much when you consider the cost of feeding your own. You will have to pay something, though.

The nicest thing is you don't have all the housing, fencing, feeding, temperaments, and smells that often come with owning one. You only need to deal with a few of those issues for the short time they are "visiting."

Artificial Insemination (AI)

As with borrowing, AI makes it's nice not to go through the hassle of keeping the males. You don't even have the short "stay" at your homestead.

This is better suited to a larger animal like a cow. You can do it for goats, but I wouldn't want to. The bucks aren't that much of a hassle. With AI you'll need to:

- Pay someone to do it for you (unless you learn how to do it yourself).
- Pay for the straws
- Learn how to detect heat in the females—which can be difficult.

Which Option Is Best?

It depends on your situation. Having a neighbor sounds like the best to me. Someone has to be that neighbor though, and if you live out in a rural area like we do, there aren't many, if any, of them.

It also depends on which of the animals we're talking about. Roosters are easy to keep and that's what you'll end up having if you want to breed chickens. Bucks and rams are smaller and easier to keep, too. When it come to a bull, most homesteaders are going to find a neighbor or do AI.

Chapter 19: Natural Remedies & Animal Health on the Homestead

Preventing sickness is always best. To keep your animals in good health is better than trying to heal them. Rotating ruminants on grass—with chickens—is great for their health. Keeping their water clean is also important. There's a time though, when no matter how good a job you do, you get a sick animal.

At this point, you have two options: call the vet or treat them yourself.

Sadly, there isn't much information online about how to treat animals naturally. There may be some, but it's not much and it's hard to find. The little advice you do find is to call the vet.

I Am *NOT* a Vet!

I am *not* a vet! I'm just a fellow homesteader who's tried a few natural remedies on our animals. I'm writing about what I've learned for two reasons:
1. If you can not call a vet or they won't come to your house for some reason, you'll have a few ideas you can try.
2. If you'd rather try a natural remedy before you call a vet, you have a few options. If you have a vet who will come to you, it's a good idea to have his name and number where you can find it, in case you ever need it.

DISCLAIMER: I'm going to show you what I've learned. This is a hard subject to write about. The following information is what has worked for me. I'm **not** a vet or animal doctor. Consider this section as me giving you a piece of friendly advice about what I've learned so far. I'm not done learning. Natural remedies for the backyard is something more people need to learn and write about. I'm showing you what I've learned so far and hope to write further about it on my blog as I learn more. I hope this sparks an interest in you to do more research and try to naturally treat before calling the vet.

Do You Call the Vet or Treat the Sick Animal Yourself?

This is a difficult question, and it's one you have to decide for yourself.

Most people will err either on one extreme or the other. You don't need to call the vet for every tiny thing, and yet you should be able to call one if you need to. Here are a few questions you can use to determine what's best to do in your situation:

- How valuable is the sick animal? All my animals are valuable to me. I want to be a good steward of every single one of them. However, there's a difference between a long-time proven milk goat and one of her bucks we're planning to eat. I care about both, but one is potentially going to give us milk for years. This doesn't mean I'd never call the vet for a buck, it's just something to consider.
- How sick is he? This, too, is important. Is your goat up, walking around and eating? He may have a problem, but how bad does he look?
- How hard is it to get the vet out to your place? If you know the vet might not come out, you need an alternative. Better to do something than nothing.

Consider all of the above. Ultimately you're going to have to make the decision. I can't make it for you. *It's your responsibility.*

Personally, I'm going to treat our animals before calling a vet in most cases. I've had goats get sick a few times—mastitis twice and diarrhea once—and was able to use natural remedies. They all worked! However, it was like walking on pins and needles until they got better. I was hoping and praying I did everything right and trusting God for the rest. I was so glad when they were better! The results I've had with my natural remedies have been great, and I plan to keep using them. There may come a time I decide it would be wiser to call the vet. I'm not opposed to using a vet if I need one. It would be good to find a local vet now, ahead of time, so you have a name and phone number ready if you need it.

Fundamental Remedy Ingredients

There are a few things you probably have around your house which are great for a sick animal. Let's look at each ingredient and see what you can use them for. Then you'll know why and how I chose the ingredients I did for the recipes to follow. Also, you may come up with your own remedy concoctions from this information. If it's an emergency and you have different ingredients on hand, this may be helpful.

Garlic

Garlic is an amazing all-around healer. It's great for a huge number of things including the few listed below. Garlic is:

- Antibacterial
- Antiviral (which means it helps with infections and viruses)
- A worm preventative and a treatment
- An egg laying stimulant for chickens

(When feeding garlic to your animals, crush it in a garlic press or blend it in a little water and mix it in their food. It may take them a little getting used to before they like it.)

Apple Cider Vinegar

ACV is our family's abbreviation for, *Apple Cider Vinegar*. Like garlic, apple cider vinegar is great for over-all health. Feed this whenever one of your animals isn't feeling well. The "good" apple cider vinegar:

- Is full of probiotics
- Is a great energy booster
- Improves digestion
- Supports the immune system
- Is great for aches and sprains
- Is high in lots of minerals, including a high amount of potassium
- Increases calcium and other mineral absorption
- Helps with respiratory health in chickens

> **Get the "Good" Apple Cider Vinegar**
> When you buy apple cider vinegar, make sure it's raw, unfiltered, and "with the mother." That's the good kind. The other is pasteurized and doesn't contain any probiotics.

> **Feeding Kefir Grains**
> I wanted to feed my goats kefir with the grains. Sadly the grains were too big to fit through my feeding syringe. I tried it a couple of times, but it didn't work well. They kept getting stuck. I skip the grains now and only use strained kefir. (You can also try blending the grains with the milk.)

Yogurt & Kefir

I heard of feeding yogurt to goats in *Storey's Guide To Raising Dairy Goats*.[1] They said to feed yogurt for the probiotics, which are great for the rumen of a sick goat. Yogurt and kefir contain lots of probiotics. We don't usually have yogurt on hand, so I used what we had—kefir. Kefir has different probiotics, but they're still great. The important thing is to feed probiotics. (The book also said you could buy probiotic capsules and feed them to your goats instead. It's easier and much less expensive to use homemade kefir or yogurt.)

Coconut Oil

Coconut oil is great for fighting infections. I've used it to fight eye infections and mastitis (which is caused by an infection in the udder). It's good for other things—but so far, I love it as a cure for infections.

Vitamin C

This is the only one I've listed here that isn't in any of the recipes to follow. That being said, it would be a good one to add to all of the oral remedies. If nothing else, feed it separately. Vitamin C is great for the immune system.

My favorite kind of vitamin C for people and animals is the kind you make out of dehydrated and blended citrus peels. It's cheap, healthy and has a higher absorption than synthetic vitamin C. *(See page 181)*

Molasses or High Energy Blend

Molasses is great for the health of the rumen (the first stomach in cows, sheep and goats, etc.). The sugars in molasses help them digest their food, and it's loaded with vitamins, minerals and nutrients. If your soil is deficient in minerals, this would be a good supplement.

High energy blend[2] from *Lancaster Agriculture* is a mix of molasses, apple cider vinegar, kelp, several other minerals, and vitamins. I used it in one of the recipes below—in place of molasses—because it was what we had on hand. Molasses is a main ingredient.

Lavender & Peppermint Essential Oils *(external use)*

You'll find these in the salve I made for my goats when they had mastitis. It was hard to find ingredients to treat mastitis. The best I could find was lavender and peppermint, which are good for preventing it. I couldn't find anything else, so I figured I'd go with them. Since then I've heard tea tree essential oil is good for preventing mastitis. It's another option if you don't have lavender or peppermint on hand. *(Use caution with essential oils and your animals. Research and know what you're doing before using them in other ways on your animals.)*

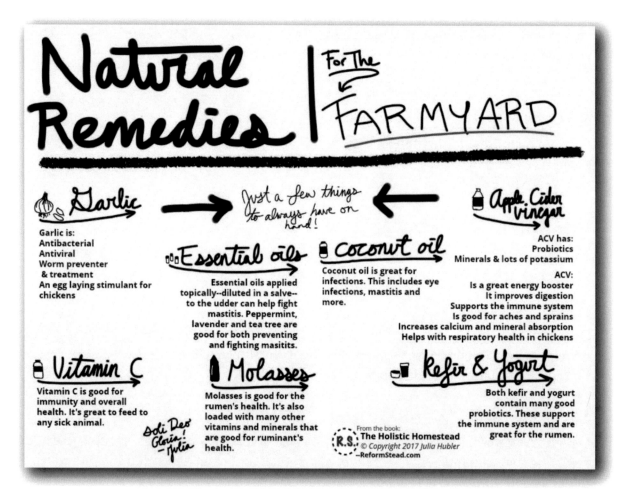

Specific Remedies & Recipes

Eye Infection Remedy

There's a simple and effective remedy for eye infections. I applied it to a meat cow we had several years back.

She had an infection around her eye when we first brought her home. It was puffy and a tannish color. I wish I had a picture to show you, but sadly I don't. The guy who helped us with her said he'd seen it in his cows before and it always went away on it's own. My mom suggested applying coconut oil for it's infection fighting properties—so I tried it.

She was a wild cow and didn't like me messing with her eye. I did it a few times and then stopped. It definitely helped the few times I was able to apply it.

Coconut oil helped our cow, so I applied it to our rabbits. A few years ago we were breeding rabbits. If the kits—baby rabbits—don't open their eyes 10 days after birth, you need to help them. The reason they can't open their eyes is usually because of an eye infection. It's important you take care of it fast, so they don't become blind.

When they were 10 days old, some of the kits got eye infections. It was in and on their eye, sealing the eye closed with a bunch of yucky, crusty gook. I applied coconut oil. They had 100% recovery! I love how easy it is to use, and how well it works.

How to Apply It—Take a generous amount of virgin coconut oil and apply it liberally to the infected area. Gently rub and massage the area as you're applying it.

Repeat this procedure 2-3 times a day, until the infection is gone and the swelling and redness are down.

The top eye is swollen closed from the infection. After applying coconut oil to an eye infection for one day his eyes are open. He's well on his way to recovery. The kit —baby rabbit—is about 10 days old here. *(Left)*

General Sick Goat Remedy

I used this recipe for one of my goats who had diarrhea. He wasn't eating much and looked more sad than normal. I still don't know what caused it. I picked a few things that are good for his rumen and immunity, and then I mixed them up into this remedy.

A feeding syringe makes giving your animals oral remedies a much easier job. The mixture in this pic is the "sick goat remedy". *(To the left)*

- 1/4 cup molasses or High Energy Blend from *Lancaster Agriculture* [2]
- 1/4 cup milk kefir, preferably made with your own raw milk
- 2-4 tablespoons raw, unfiltered apple cider vinegar
- 1 clove of garlic, crushed as small as possible so you can get it through the syringe.

Mix everything together in a small canning jar or a mug. After it's mixed, draw up about 30-40 cc's (That's about 3-5 Tablespoons, or 40-80 millimeters) in a feeding syringe.

Feed it to your sick goat three times a day until he is better.

Naturally Treating Mastitis—*Our Story*

Two things I've found are amazing for treating mastitis:

1. A salve you apply to the udder.
2. A natural remedy "medicine" you mix up and feed to her orally.

I've dealt with two cases of mastitis in our goats. The first one was mild. The salve alone got rid of it.

The second case was more challenging. I was glad I had already helped one goat through a milder round of it. I knew a little about what to do. This case of mastitis was ten times worse than the first one. She's the reason I came up with the second remedy. The salve alone wasn't working well enough, or as fast as it should have. The combination of the two remedies worked best.

I'm going to give you my recipes for the salve and an oral remedy in a minute. First let me show you the symptoms and conditions of my goats' mastitis. See how it compares to your situation, and how I used the remedies I made.

Our First Mastitis Case—Our first goat got mastitis shortly after we bought her. She was the second goat I was milking and I think she may have gotten it from me being a new milker. I'm not sure, but it's a possibility.

One morning as I was milking, I noticed I couldn't milk her all the way out. I didn't know why, and I didn't know what was going on.

I put her away half-milked. *Bad idea!* I never should have done that! I should have figured things out and finished milking her, but I didn't. Learn from my mistake! Leaving the milk in your goat will only make things worse. I hate to say it, but I want you to know what was going on and learn from my mistake—*never do this!*

Later, my mom helped me research it. She suggested it might be mastitis. After I knew what it might be, I tried to find remedies for it online. It was hard. I found great stuff on how to prevent mastitis, but how helpful was that then? My goat had it. I needed a remedy, not ways to prevent it.

I made a salve for her udder. I found a few essential oils which were recommended to prevent mastitis—it was the best I could do. I went with lavender and peppermint essential oils in the salve.

After making it, I massaged it onto her udder before and while I was milking. I noticed it helped a lot right away. As I was milking, I pulled out as many milk clots as possible, and I was able to milk her all the way out. The clots of milk softened and came out better with the salve.

She got all the way better *and fast!* I was so glad. She's now fully recovered and hasn't had it since.

Don't Drink Milk From a Sick Goat...

If your goat has mastitis, clumpy milk, streaks of blood in the milk,
or if she's sick—don't drink it. Feed it to the chickens. They'll love it and you
won't have to waste it.

Note: Only feed your chickens milk if you're treating your goats naturally. Don't feed your chickens
milk from a goat you're treating with conventional antibiotics. The antibiotics may get in the milk
and you don't want to feed that to your animals.

Our Second Goat's Mastitis Was Worse—Our second goat's mastitis was worse and more complicated than the first case. I took detailed notes when she had it, so I'm able to go into more detail.

You'd think, since we already had one goat with mastitis, I would've recognized it sooner—sadly, no.

She was in her first lactation when she got it. She was a cruel mama to her newborn kids—so mean that we had to separate them. I had to tie the mama up to let her kids nurse. (Bottle feeding sounded like too much work.) After about a week, I was milking some for our family and letting the kids nurse. About 25 days after she freshened, I realized she had been developing mastitis over the last few days or even weeks.

She had been extremely hard to milk, and when I first noticed it, I thought it was my hands not used to milking—*I just needed to get into practice again.* Then I noticed there was a tiny bit of blood on my hand. I looked at her and found she had something like blisters on the tips of her teats. I felt bad for milking her so firmly! I slowed down and milked her more slowly and gently—it took a long time to get all the milk out. Her udder and teats were *hard*.

I realized she was having mastitis issues and I applied the mastitis salve I used on our other goat. Two days later there were large lumps I could feel in her udder. They wouldn't come out because they were too big, and they always got in the way and blocked the milk from coming out. I'm not sure when I noticed them—she also had streaks of blood in the milk clots.

Next morning she was sick. She looked sad, with a droopy face and eyes, and she wouldn't eat anything. That evening she ate a little and seemed better than she was in the morning. I made an ACV udder wash—recipe below—which I used to "rinse" her udder.

I also applied coconut oil to her udder and put some coconut oil around her mouth so she'd lick it off. I figured it would be good for her to ingest, too.

Then I realized I could use a syringe and get "healthy remedies" in her. I used the syringes we use ourselves for cod liver oil. It took six times to get all of my "oral mastitis remedy" in her.

She liked the mixture, but hated how many times I stuck the syringe in her mouth. (Due to the tiny syringe we had.) I *highly* recommend getting a feeding syringe (see picture on page 138). They're bigger and much easier to use. I also added a little apple cider vinegar to her water bucket for her to drink.

She was way better the next day. In the evening I was able to pull/work out all the lumps of milk that had been in her udder for the last few days. They shrunk, softened, and finally came out. *It was so much easier to milk after that!*

After milking I used the ACV Udder Wash again. Then I massaged in some coconut oil. I gave her my oral mastitis remedy and put some apple cider vinegar in her water.

The next day I didn't have problems with lumps in her milk—her mastitis was pretty much better. I kept up the same treatment for the next few days to make sure she was fine and tapered her off the treatments.

Oral Remedy for a Goat With Mastitis *(Oral Mastitis Remedy)*

This is similar to the *"sick goat remedy"*. This recipe makes the right amount for one dose.

- 1 tablespoon milk kefir
- 1 teaspoon coconut oil, melted
- 1 teaspoon apple cider vinegar, *raw, unfiltered and "with the mother"*

Mix everything together in a mug or small glass jar. Feed *all of it* to your goat in a feeding syringe. Repeat twice a day until she's better. Continue feeding it a few days after the symptoms are gone, just to be safe.

Mastitis Salve—*Remedy*

A wonderful mastitis preventative or treatment. This salve softens the udder and loosens milk clots. Use it every day or as needed.

Makes about 2/3 cup

- 3 Tablespoon shredded beeswax, packed tightly
- 3 Tablespoons shea butter
- 2 Tablespoons coconut oil
- 2 Tablespoons olive oil
- 24 drops lavender essential oil
- 12 drops peppermint essential oil

Place a small-medium pot on the stove with about an inch of water in the bottom. Turn on high and bring to a boil.

In the meantime, place the beeswax, shea butter, coconut oil, and olive oil in a glass measuring cup. (Put the beeswax on the bottom so it melts faster.)

When the water boils, turn the stove down to low-medium. Place the measuring cup in the water. Occasionally, mix with a spoon until everything is melted and clear. Take the measuring cup out and set it on the counter.

Add in the essential oils and stir. (When mixing in the essential oils, if the liquid salve is too hot, the essential oils may evaporate. It helps to let it cool a little—just make sure to add them before it cools too much and hardens.) Pour into a glass jar or tin—preferably one with a lid.

To Use:
Scoop some out with your fingers and massage onto your goat's—or cow's—udder. Rub the extras into your hands or bring a rag to wipe off the leftover salve.

Tips:
* You can also use lavender and peppermint essential oils in your favorite salve recipe instead of this one—if you'd prefer.
* If you want to use a different essential oil, I've heard tea tree is also good for mastitis.

ACV Udder Wash Recipe

This recipe can be used on a regular basis to clean and sterilize the udder. It keeps bacteria out of the milk duct minimizing the chance of mastitis (or in my case, helping it). There's a lot of good probiotics—and more—to help too.

- 1 tablespoon apple cider vinegar, *raw, unfiltered, and "with the mother."*
- 1/2 cup of water

Mix them together in a bucket. Take a rag and wipe as much as you can onto your goats udder *(without double-dipping)*. Do this several times—with a clean rag each time—as a wash for the udder.

Then milk the goat as usual. When you're done, apply salve or coconut oil.

If You Don't Have a Feeding Syringe

Oral medicine syringes—made for people—can be used for your goats in a pinch, though it isn't ideal. You have to squirt it in their mouth over and over again to feed them the full dose. They don't like it, but it works when needed.

I used these to feed my milk goat when she got mastitis because I didn't have anything else. Long-term, I recommend getting a feeding syringe[3]. It's way easier for you and your goat. I bought one big enough for our cow and it works great for the goats, too. (If you use a syringe for your animals, set it aside and don't use it for your family.)

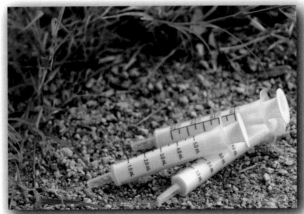

ACV in Your Goats Water

It's easy to add apple cider vinegar (ACV) to your goat's water. It has many valuable properties that can help mastitis or other sicknesses.

Make sure the water is clean, then add about 1/2 cup apple cider vinegar to every 5 gallons of water. (Or you can eyeball it. I never measure.) Keep their water clean and replace the water with ACV daily.

I Found Another Idea—*(After Our Goats Had Mastitis)*

"Apply hot wet towels and massage the udder to break up clots. Alternate hot towels with stripping. There is a fine description of this treatment by James Herriot in *All Creatures Great and Small*. A poor and desperate farmer had a cow with such a bad case of mastitis that Herriot expected to find her dead by the next morning. But the man sat by his cow all through the night stripping out milk and applying hot towels (supplied, no doubt, by his equally sleepless wife). In the morning when Herriot returned, the cow was fully recovered." —*Keeping A Family Milk Cow* [4]

The Holistic Chicken Health Guide

"An ounce of prevention is worth a pound of cure,"—chickens health included. Keep your chickens as healthy as possible and you may never have any major sickness to worry about.

The "Everything Remedy" for Chickens

One thing you can do to improve your chickens health is to feed them *garlic and apple cider vinegar!*

You'll prevent sickness, worms, infections, and more in your chickens. (Plus garlic is an egg laying stimulant! Meaning garlic will encourage your hens to lay more eggs. Who doesn't want that?!)

Chickens *love* garlic and apple cider vinegar. They may have to get used to it though—then garlic and apple cider vinegar will be their favorite treat!

I feed garlic and apple cider vinegar whenever they seem sick. If one dies and it could be disease related, I add it to the rest of my chickens' water. It's a great precaution, and it's great for their immune system.

How to Feed Garlic & Apple Cider Vinegar

Add crushed, fresh garlic and apple cider vinegar to their water. While you're first introducing it, start out giving them less, and over a week or two work up to the full amount.

For the first few days start with 1 clove of crushed garlic and 2 tablespoons of apple cider vinegar. Work up to 3 cloves of garlic and about 1/4 cup of apple cider vinegar (for 10 liters of water). You don't need to measure it unless you want to. I always take a guess. The exact numbers aren't that important, as long as you're in the ballpark.

How often do you feed it? Feed it to them when you want to give them an extra health boost or if they're sick. As a preventative you can feed it once a week, once a month, or however often you desire.

Herbs for Chickens

Herbs are amazing for your chickens' health.

- **Alfalfa** is full of lots of protein, amino acids, and minerals. This is a great food to grow for chickens. (Alfalfa is a common GMO crop. Make sure you get non-GMO alfalfa and/or seeds.)

- **Basil** is antibacterial, and can be used for mucous membrane health.

- **Cilantro** is good for bone health, has antioxidant properties, helps keep fungus away and is high in Vitamins A and K (which are good for eye health and blood clotting).

- **Comfrey** is very high in protein, calcium, potassium and amino acids. Comfrey is a herb I have been wanting to grow for years and haven't gotten to yet. There are so many good things to be said about it. It is a controversial herb though. Some say it is bad to feed to chickens, yet others say it's the best thing in the world. Look it up for yourself. I've decided if it's one plant in a holistic garden with other food sources, it's fine for them to eat.

- **Dandelions** are full of amazing minerals but it is considered a weed in many places. You can give your chickens the whole plant—a great source of green food.

- **Dill** helps with respiratory health, is a sedative/relaxant, and contains antioxidant properties.

- **Fennel Seed** is an egg laying stimulant.

- **Garlic** is antibacterial, antiviral, and an egg laying stimulant.

- **Lavender** lowers stress and is an insect repellent.

- **Lemon Balm** lowers stress, repels rodents and is antibacterial.

- **Marigold** is an egg laying stimulant.

- **Marjoram** is another egg laying stimulant.

- **Nasturtium** is yet another egg laying stimulant. Also, it is an antibiotic, antiseptic, insecticide, and de-wormer.

- **Nettles** are full of calcium, protein, phosphorus, potassium, and magnesium. A great green food to grow in your garden.

- **Oregano** has antibiotics that may prevent infections, e-coli, salmonella, avian flu and black head.

- **Parsley** is rich in vitamins and is an egg laying stimulant.

- **Peppermint** is an insect repellent and parasite control.

- **Rose Petals** are high in vitamin C.

- **Rosemary** is an insect repellant, and is good for pain relief and respiratory health.

- **Sage** helps control parasites and is an antioxidant.

- **Thyme** is great for respiratory health and parasite control. Also, it is an antioxidant and antibacterial.

- **Wormwood** is a dewormer, plus it helps in lice control and general health.

How to Feed Chickens Herbs

The best way to feed chickens herbs is to plant them right outside their coop. The chickens harvest and eat them whenever they desire. Include herbs in a chicken garden or grow a few around their coop. *(See Chapter 8.)*

The other feeding option requires more work on your end. Pick herbs and add them to their nesting boxes, dust baths, coop floor, chicken feed, or hang some in the coop.

There are so many herbs you can plant. Pick a few and start! In the long run you want many different species of herbs in your chicken garden. This is the holistically minded approach.

Conclusion...

I hope this brief chapter on natural remedies was helpful. I plan to write more about this topic on my website if/when I come up with more natural remedies for my animals.

You may decide to ignore this whole section and move on. That's fine. Just remember, I'm not a vet. I'm showing you what has worked for me. *You* need to decide if you're going to try it.

Chapter 20: Fly Control & Prevention

If you don't have any flies or have never had any—ahhhh—yeah right! Flies are a constant up-hill battle.

Try as you might, everyone has or will go through seasons of flies. As I type, it seems we have a plague of flies! Almost every time we have a problem, I can trace it back to mismanagement. I should have had the chickens in with the cow and the compost pile, and then we might not have had so many flies right now.

This chapter is more than the simple fly spray recipe. I've got no problem with fly sprays. I've heard they're great. It's just not the main point of this chapter. We're going to dig deeper and get to the root of the problem. We'll talk about prevention and then go over the options you have for natural controls.

Why flies?! Where do they come from?

It All Goes Back to Management

The fly lays its eggs in garbage, manure or dead rotting things. The eggs soon hatch into white maggots. After about 2-5 days these turn into a reddish-brown pupae. Your goal is to have your chickens to eat them before they turn into adult flies.

Proper management helps keep fly populations down. Another thing to consider is, *are they coming from your property or your neighbor's?* If they're coming from your neighbor, it'll be difficult no matter what you do. When they're coming from your place, you have much more control.

Get to the Source & Prevent Flies

It's difficult, but possible. First you need to find where they're laying their eggs. They like to lay their eggs in:

- Garbage
- Compost (if not properly composting)
- Dead or rotting things
- Manure

Garbage—is smelly and flies are attracted to that. Compost as much of it as you can. If you need to have trash on your homestead until it gets picked up or you take it to the dump, keep it in a closed container.

Compost—that's not decomposing correctly can be an issue. If the compost smells bad, something is wrong. Flies love the bad smells and want to lay their eggs there. Have the right balance of carbon, nitrogen, water and oxygen in the compost, and let your chickens help with it. They'll tear down the pile and eat any fly larvae they find. You'll need to re-stack the pile after they tear it down, but you'll need to turn it anyway. If they aren't interested in the compost, sprinkle a little of their chicken food on it. They'll get the idea.

Rotting Things—shouldn't be laying around your homestead. This will obviously cause problems.

Manure—is a problem if not managed well. When properly managed, manure provides no fly problems and huge benefits to the homestead. There are two ways to properly manage manure: either compost it or let the chickens spread it on your pasture.

If your animals are penned up, scoop their manure out every day and compost it. If you're rotating (or free-ranging) your ruminants on pasture, let the chickens follow them. As they do, they'll eat the fly larvae and bugs. Then they'll spread the natural fertilizer.

> **"If the manure is properly handled it will never smell."** —*Joel Salatin* [1]

How to Control Flies Naturally

Prevention is the priority. However, there are times when things get a little out of hand. The problem may be on your homestead or a neighbor's. Either way, you may want to consider a natural fly *remedy*.

There are many options for controlling flies. Just don't start here and miss *prevention!* Preventing always works better than trying to get rid of them.

Natural Homemade Fly Sprays

I haven't used these yet. They look like they'd be nice if there are lots of flies when you're milking. If/when I make a fly spray recipe, I'd go to ReformationAcres.com or ThePrairieHomestead.com. Both have great looking recipes.

Fly Traps

These are another option. (It seems a waste of time to me, you'll never get all the flies. Prevention seems more worth your time. There are times they can help though.) We've used fly traps in the past. Buy one from the store or make one.[2]

Fly Masks for Cows

There's a great way to keep flies out of your cow's eyes—use a fly mask. Cows are susceptible to pink eye, so keeping flies away from their eyes is a *priority*.

Maggot Buckets As Prevention & Control

Use maggot buckets for prevention and longer-term fly control. The principle of maggot buckets is simple. Put rotten meat in a bucket with holes in the bottom.

The flies come for the smell, lay their eggs, and the maggots crawl out the bottom. The key is to have the bucket in a location where the chickens will eat the fallen maggots. *(See page 94)*

How does this prevent flies on your homestead? When the fly lays her eggs in the location you've chosen for the "chicken food," there will be that many less flies on your homestead because the chickens will eat them before they have the chance to come to become pesky adults.

Chapter 21: Holistic Points Applied...

I want to say a quick word about a few more things before concluding Part 2. Let's take a brief look at a few odds and ends you may have, get, or do, now or in the future.

Meat Chickens

A lot of people raise broilers. They're fairly cheap and easy to start with, and the turnover is quick. It's about 8-12 weeks till butchering, depending on the breed.

They're next on our list of animals to get. We plan to raise them in a chicken tractor and rotate them behind the cow and goats on pasture. They'll eat bugs, grass and manure from the cow and goats. They're a great fit in the holistic picture.

Sheep

Sheep are ruminants, as are cows and goats. There are lots of similarities between them. There are also some distinctions. The most important difference is *how* they eat and benefit your pasture. *(See Chapter 4)*

Rabbits

Rabbits can provide a lot of meat for little cost. They're small enough that even a city dweller can raise them.

Rabbits can have 8-10 kits (baby rabbits) in a litter and 7-8 litters a year. This means for every doe you have, you have the potential of 56-80 rabbits a year! You can either butcher or sell them, but that's a lot of meat. They don't eat much and only take a little space. If you wanted you could make a cage—with a chicken wire floor—and rotate them on pasture.

We raised rabbits for a few years. We live in the desert and 120+ degree days are a regular occurrence. Although we took measures to keep them cool, it wasn't enough. They do better with a cooler climate. As long as you provide protection from wind, rain and snow, they can stand temperatures well below freezing.

Weeds Can Be Grown and Fed to Your Rabbits

You can cut your feed costs completely by growing weeds for your rabbits. Find out which weeds are safe for rabbits in your area. Also, if you don't have weeds you can save money on pelleted feed by feeding alfalfa. Although it is a little less convenient, it's cheaper. (The pellets are almost 100% alfalfa anyway.) Buy a bale for them like you would for your goats. *It'll last a lot longer though.*

Pigs

When I think of raising pigs, I think of reading about how small towns would raise their pigs by letting them roam free in the woods. Here's a quote from a book written by Sergeant Alvin York *(1887-1964)*. He lived in the back woods of Tennessee before he became an important figure in World War I, and he says this about raising pigs:

"We keep hogs in the woods all the time. They get fat on the acorns, beechnuts, hickory nuts, and chestnuts. They jes grub around and find them or dig them up and have a right-smart time. Sometimes as many as fifty different farmers have their hogs running in the same woods. We all mark them with our own particular mark and fasten bells on straps around the necks of the leaders." [1]

If you have a lot of wooded land—and a fence these days—this may be a holistic option. Not everyone has that, though. *(We won't be doing this in our Arizona desert.)*

Joel Salatin has great advice for raising pigs holistically, and he has lots of great ways to fit pigs on a farm. I read a good amount about pigs in his book, *You Can Farm.* Even if you aren't "farming", you can use and apply his concepts on your homestead.

Honey Bees

Keeping bees is another potential homestead project. If you place them near the garden, they can pollinate your fruits and vegetables in addition to the honey they'll provide.

Keep in mind how many people are around since you don't want your family to get stung. Place them as far from people as possible.

[Side Note: For a long time I thought the orchard would be a great location on the homestead for honey bee hives. They would be out of the way of people, and the honey bees could pollinate the trees when they were in bloom. Then I learned honey bees aren't good at pollinating fruit trees. For successful fruit set, the pollination needs to take place early, before the honey bees are flying around. Other *kinds* of bees do a better job at pollinating your orchard flowers. The bumblebee and blue orchard bee—among many other flying insects—are some of the best pollinators for your fruit trees. *(The orchard still may be a good place for your bee hives—just not for the reason of pollinating fruit tree flowers.)]*

Dogs

You can't talk about homesteading and not discuss the importance of dogs! If you want to get a homestead dog, great! Before you go out and buy "a dog", let me warn you, not all dogs will work well with your homestead.

Think about the breed you plan to get before you buy. When you choose a breed, go with a breed that's meant to protect and help your homestead rather than harm it. For example, you can get a bird dog and attempt to train him not to do what he's been bred to do (eat birds), but plan on an up-hill battle that takes a lot if time. *(Providing you're raising chickens—which are birds.)*

Within any breed, you may end up with a dog who doesn't fit with your homestead. Do yourself a favor and at least start with a breed known to fit in with farm animals.

We have an Aussie mutt and a purebred Australian Shepherd (who my sister is planning to breed). They have their issues (like eating eggs and newly hatched chicks), but overall they have been a great protection to all of our animals. I try to make sure no chicks are where they can get them, and most of our chickens lay their eggs where the dogs can't go.

Besides Aussies there are many other breeds of herding dogs and LGD's (Livestock Guardian Dogs) that would work well on a homestead.

Cats

Cats are another farm animal not to be overlooked. Mice, ground squirrels, rodents and lizards can be controlled with a cat. Make sure your cat doesn't eat your chickens though. We haven't had one who has killed or eaten our chickens, but some will. Make a plan of what you'll do if that happens. You may want to find another home for him.

———————————————————

Butchering With a Holistic Mindset

Of course when you're butchering, the meat gets top priority. Some folks will also keep the fat and render it down into lard or tallow. After that, there are still lots of pieces leftover.

Holistic butchering finds a way to use every part and piece of the animal. I haven't figured it all out yet, but I keep my eyes open for ideas.

After butchering, feed some of the leftover scraps you won't eat to your chickens—for example, the guts, intestines, etc. (You should or can eat the heart, liver, gizzard and feet —of chickens—and the bones can be made into broth. They are very nutritious, but if you're not using them for yourselves, feed them to the chickens.)

You may need to cut or tear the parts into smaller pieces if they're large. (Chickens sometimes get lazy and like their meals cut up for them.)

When butchering large animals, your chickens may not be able to eat all you have to give them, or as fast as you'd want. In that case you may need to freeze or dispose of it before it smells or rots. (In most other cases I'd recommend freezing it. With guts and dirty stuff like that, toss them!)

There's a debate about whether or not you should feed chicken meat to other chickens. Do your own research and decide for yourself. As long as it isn't in large quantities, I'm not going to worry it.

Example: The chickens have access to our food scraps that go to the compost. There may be an occasional piece of chicken in there, but I don't feed them butchering scraps from other chickens.

Also, meat scraps, raw bones with meat on them, fat, etc. can be fed to the dogs and cat.

Butchering Scraps & Pigs

Think about what pigs would eat in the wild. Everything they can find! They eat roots, insects, wild nuts, grasses, weeds, and any *dead animals* they find or can hunt and kill. This is what you get if you shoot and eat a wild boar. It's natural for pigs to eat some meat and everything else on a dead animal.

Drawing the connections here, you can feed your pigs scraps from butchering. I've read that they've tried to chase down a calf to eat. When you butcher—any size animal—feed all of your scraps, including the gut sack, to your pigs.

Most conventional folks will disagree with me here. That's okay. It's something you need to think about and decide—it makes sense to me.

Note: After the chickens or other animals have had the scraps for a little while, pick up what they didn't eat. If left, it will breed all sorts of bad pathogens and worms that can make your animals sick—or even kill them.

Chapter 22: Make the Connections

Look around and *see* connections. When you can see them, it'll be easier for you to go out the back door and put together *your* unique puzzle pieces. That's key to an efficient, holistic homestead.

Remember the Holistic Homestead is:

A piece of land, however small or large, for which the owner *takes into account all aspects of the natural and other resources.*

He makes every piece work together in the most productive way, *for the benefit of the entire system and everything therein.*

Land, home, animals, plants and all things, down to the soil microbes—in essence every living thing—are brought under his dominion.
—from Chapter 1 of this book

This chapter is the finish line and the starting point at the same time. No matter what part of the race you're in, something here can be taken and applied to your homestead. It's a key chapter to this book and a holistic homestead.

The Larger Connections

In Chapters 4-12 we laid the ***groundwork***. We set the land in order—ready to receive animals. We got the grass growing, the microbes happy, the compost going, fruit trees planted, vegetables and herbs sprouting, and beneficial insects flying around. We set things up so some of it is watered by greywater and rainwater.

From there we went into the ***expansion***. We delved into chickens and other fowl, milk goats and cows, milking, breeding, fly prevention, and a how-to on farmyard remedies!

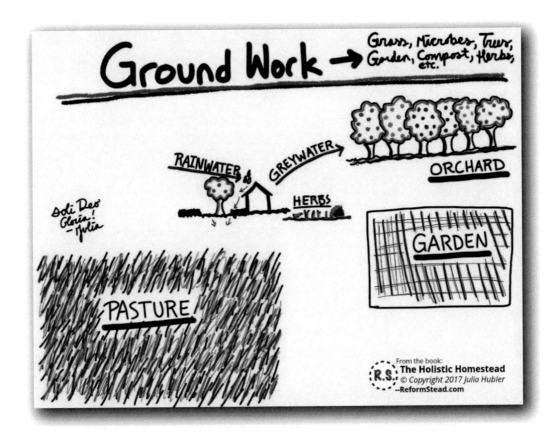

Ground Work → Grass, Microbes, Trees, Garden, Compost, Herbs, etc.

RAINWATER   GREYWATER →

ORCHARD

HERBS

GARDEN

PASTURE

Soli Deo Gloria! — Julia

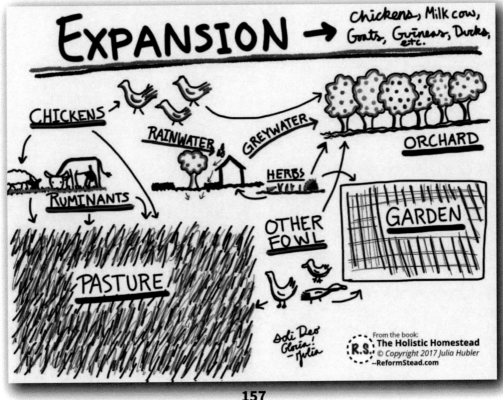

EXPANSION → Chickens, Milk cow, Goats, Guineas, Ducks, etc.

CHICKENS →

RAINWATER   GREYWATER

ORCHARD

RUMINANTS

HERBS

OTHER FOWL

GARDEN

PASTURE

Soli Deo Gloria! — Julia

That's probably not the exact order your homestead will grow. You'll probably try several things at once. We did. The "groundwork" is never perfect before you move into "expansion." The expansion makes the groundwork better. Try growing all the groundwork with only a little stir-bought manure and compost—*A holistic homestead needs both!*

Putting the Smaller Pieces Together

Although many of these connections are small, they are in no way less important. Little things can make the biggest difference. After all, your finger may be one of the "least important" parts of your body, but that doesn't mean you don't care about them. Smash one with a hammer and you'll know what I'm talking about.

Inside all of the topics we've covered are thousands of connections. Puzzle pieces waiting to be put together correctly. See how many of the following connections could be applied to your homestead—present or future.

"Well done, good and faithful servant; you were faithful over a few things, I will make you ruler over many things." —*Matthew 25:21 (NKJV)*

Your Family & Your Homestead

You and your family get to take dominion of your land and animals. Your hard work keeps everything running smoothly, provides food, and possibly income. A homestead gives lots of work for the whole family and is a great place to train your kids and give them a good work ethic. Hard work that comes with homesteading is healthy and good for you. It's not just your plants that will grow.

Grass & Your Homestead

Grass:
- Grows healthier fats in animals—meaning better food for your family.
- Gives space for rainwater to infiltrate into the soil.
- Provides healthy food for your animals.
- Grows healthier eggs and meat.
- Improves the health of your animals.

Microbes & Your Homestead

Microbes:
- Are the foundation of a healthy homestead. Healthy microbes = a healthy homestead.
- Are the foundation for plants with the most nutritional value. If you have a balanced population of microbes, you provide the best start for your plants.

Compost & Your Homestead

Compost:
- Gives your family healthier food. Fruits, vegetables, and pastured animals all grow stronger with compost.
- Gives soil lots of microbes and living organisms, which translates to more vitamins, minerals and nutrients in the vegetables and fruits harvested.
- Balances the soil food web, which, when in balance, attracts more beneficial insects and honey bees.
- Supplies the garden with organic matter.
- Provides organic matter and microbes for the garden, orchard and pasture.
- Gives the chickens food (food scraps, bugs, larva, etc).
- Puts the chickens to work—tearing down the pile.
- Gives animals cleaner living pens—when manure is composted.
- Controls bugs, flies, and parasites—when manure is composted.
- Is a clean solution for manure.
- Applied to grass, means better food for ruminants, and is amazing for every inch of the homesteader's soil.
- Means less trash in the kitchen and fewer garbage bags used.

Fruit Trees, the Garden & Your Homestead

Trees & Garden:
- Provide healthy fruits and vegetables for your family.
- Provide chopped or ground up dead garden plant matter to lay on the soil as mulch to keep the microbes healthy. (Wood chips and leaves in the orchard.)
- Grow carbon (aka: straw, organic matter, etc.) for your compost.
- Provide dead plants, stalks, and leaves that can be composted.
- Provide food for beneficial insects and honey bees.
- Provide a solution and a place for greywater.
- Grow fruits and vegetables to feed to your chickens.
- Put a flock of chickens to work cleaning up after harvest.

- Put chickens to work spreading a pile of mulch. (Organic matter, wood chips, straw, compost, etc.)
- Feed chickens and put them to work eating bugs.
- Grow greens, grains and vegetables for your milk animals.
- Provide food for your animals. Pumpkins, carrots, beets and more can be grown for cattle, sheep, goats, rabbits and pigs. *Great for over-winter fodder.*
- Feed ruminants yummy treats such as the leftover beet and carrot tops you don't want. Also, you can grow lettuce, kale, spinach, etc., specifically for them to eat.
- Provide apple trimmings (and other goat-edible trees) that can be fed to your goats.

Herbs & Your Homestead

Herbs:
- Provide natural remedies and health for your family.
- Give diversity to the microbes in the soil.
- Provide diversity to the garden and tree guilds.
- Repel pests, including flies, with their strong smell.
- Attract beneficial insects.
- Provide pollen and nectar—food for the bees.
- Provide natural remedies and health care for chickens, fowl cows, sheep and goats.

Weeds & Your Homestead

Weeds:
- Are often edible and can be eaten by your family.
- Are better than nothing. The microbes need roots to inoculate so they can thrive.
- Mine up minerals and do so much more for the trees they grow near. It's best to plant good weeds like dandelions.
- Attract beneficial insects and honey bees to their flowers.
- Can be fed to your chickens, geese, ducks and muscovies.
- Are a favorite food for goats.
- Can have medicinal properties.
- Can be grown and fed to your rabbits and pigs.

Beneficial Insects & Your Homestead

"Good Bugs":
- Are evidence your microbes are growing healthy.
- Provide pollination to the garden and trees.
- Are pest control for your garden. They eat the bad bugs.

Rainwater, Greywater & Your Homestead

Rain & Greywater:
- Enable you to use less fresh water which saves you money.
- Can help feed your family through the fruit you grow with it.
- Make a homestead greener, with plants that grow stronger.
- Transforms another kitchen and whole household "waste" into a resource.

Chickens & Your Homestead

Chickens:
- Feed your family with eggs and/or meat.
- Use up the food "wastes" from your kitchen—food scraps, milk, etc.
- Help turn the compost pile—letting in needed oxygen.
- Eat unwanted bugs and larva out of the compost.
- Add nitrogen to compost.
- Use their manure in your compost for your garden.
- Clean up the garden after you harvest.
- Eat extra and overripe produce from the garden.
- Spread a pile of mulch, wood chips, straw, etc.
- Provide pest and bug control for the homestead, grass, garden, orchard, etc. Ticks, scorpions and many other bugs are easily controlled by even a small flock of chickens.
- Act as manure spreaders—letting it absorb into the grass.
- Provide fertilizer for the grass and garden.
- Provide parasite control for your grass and ruminants.
- Eat some of your butchering scraps.
- Provide fly prevention by eating the larva in manure before they turn into flies.
- Provide sanitation for rabbits by cleaning up after them.

Guineas, Ducks, Geese, Turkeys & Your Homestead

Other Fowl:
- Provide your family with eggs and meat while giving you many benefits such as the ones listed below.
    - Guineas eat lots of many kinds of bugs, especially ants, while leaving the plants and garden produce alone.
    - Geese eat mostly grass and are great at cleaning up fallen fruit in the orchard.
    - Geese can protect the chickens in the pasture from aerial predators.

- Muscovies are great grazers, but they also eat lots of bugs, slugs and worms.
- Ducks are known to eat lots of snails, slugs, and insects.
- Turkeys like insects, grains, and greens.

Milk Cows, Goats & Your Homestead

Milk Cows & Goats:
- Give milk and meat (if you raise their babies) to your family.
- Provide manure which is a great source of nitrogen for the compost pile or garden.
- Provide fertilizer for the grass and pasture.
- Eat weeds around your homestead and pasture. (Goats)
- "Mow" your pasture. (Cows)
- Improve the pasture with rotational grazing.
- Provide manure which is a food source for the chickens.
- Provide "dirty" milk for the chickens *when* the goat or cow steps in it.

Pigs & Your Homestead

Pigs:
- Provide your family with meat and lots of lard (a healthy cooking fat).
- Give you a place to throw all your food scraps.
- Are a water saver for the septic—rinse the dishes into a bucket and feed them the "dirty" food-water.
- Can turn soil, compost, animals' bedding, etc.
- Can be raised on pasture without tearing it up if you get the right breed.
- Are a garbage disposal since everything leftover from butchering can be fed to them.

Rabbits & Your Homestead

Rabbits:
- Give lots of cheap, easy to raise meat for your family.
- Provide manure that can be composted or applied directly to the garden. Unlike most manures, rabbit manure won't burn your plants like others will.
- Are easy to feed since pasture can be cut and fed to them, or they can be rotated on it.
- Provide another source of food for chickens since chickens can go under the rabbit cages to clean up the manure.
- Provide meat scraps from butchering (guts, etc.) that can be fed to the chickens. Rabbits are small, so even a small flock of chickens can eat all of the butchering scraps of one rabbit.

Broilers & Your Homestead

Broilers:
- Provide inexpensive, high quality, fast meat for your family.
- Provide manure that can be turned into compost or used to fertilize the pasture.
- Can be rotated behind the ruminants to provide parasite, fly, and bug control.

Sheep & Your Homestead

Sheep:
- Provide grass-fed meat and occasionally, milk for your family.
- Improve pasture by eating it low and fertilizing it.
- Provide manure—food for the chickens to eat.

Bees & Your Homestead

Bees:
- Give you honey and wax.
- Provide pollination for your fruits and vegetables.

Dogs & Your Homestead

Dogs:
- Guard your other animals and keep them safe from predators. (In my opinion every one of our chickens owes their life to our first Aussie, Sammy.)
- Can protect your family and children too.
- May help scare off some of the critters who want to eat your garden.

Cats & Your Homestead

Cats:
- Are great at controlling small critters like mice.
- Can eat leftover milk and/or food scraps from your kitchen.

Butchering & Your Homestead

Butchering:
- Provides your family with healthy, clean meat.
- Provides scraps that can be fed to the chickens, pigs, dogs and cats.

The Kitchen & Your Homestead

Kitchen:

- Provides leftovers, food scraps, vegetables, fruits & old food that can be fed to the chickens, pigs, dogs or cats.
- Provides moldy food for the compost. (Don't compost meat, eggs, milk, oil or fat).
- Provides greywater from the kitchen sink to water fruit and shade trees.
- Provides storage for milk (in the freezer) for orphan kids or calves.

Connection Examples:

Hopefully by now you can see there are *thousands* of connections you can make, and pieces you can put together. I want to give you two examples:

Example #1—The chickens turn and add to the compost, and the compost goes to your garden's microbes. The microbes grow strong, and make the plants grow better. The plants and vegetables have more vitamins and minerals. You eat the vegetables, and the scraps go to the compost pile. The chickens eat what scraps they want and the cycle starts again.

Example #2—You do all you can to grow healthy grass. You get a cow and rotate her on the pasture. The sheep follow her and eat the shorter grass. The chickens are next and eat the fly larvae, bad bugs and parasites, and then they spread the fertilizer around and leave a little extra behind. Then the pasture rests, and the fertilizer soaks in. The microbes are in optimal health. The grass grows tall—and we're right back where we started.

Do you see where I'm going with this? Those "lists" which fill this chapter aren't dry and boring. *See them as a place to start seeing and making the connections!*

Don't stop here! Those are just the few I saw. Consider it a launch-pad to start your own connection-making journey.

Remember—*think holistically.*

---> Part 3 <---

Indoor Homesteading

Chapter 23: Connections in the Home...

We've made connections outside, now it's time to make them inside. Many of the same rules apply inside that apply outside.

We need to put all the pieces together just like in the earlier chapters—only now inside. We want the whole homestead to work together. We need to make connections.

As we go through Part 3, you'll notice the connections often start in the home and go outside. Food scraps go *out* to the chickens, and eggs come *in* for breakfast—it all connects back *outside*.

Save Money

Learn to use what you have by finding what most people call junk and turn it into a resource. Find ways to save money and be resourceful.

Example: Collect glass jars. Instead of tossing, reuse them. They're cheaper than canning jars and often work as well for storage. (Use canning jars for canning.)

Although none of the chapters are titled *"How to Save Money"*, the topic is still covered. Reducing waste is a big way to save and so are efficient systems. Saving money on food and in the kitchen is more than getting the best deal at the grocery store.

Learn New Skills—*Outside Too!*

There are always new skills to learn. After mastering one, find another. Add to your list of skills and things you can do.

Most folks don't know how to do very basic things. They have their profession and pay others to do the rest. You need to teach yourself to learn—and fail. You're *learning*—not knowing. The knowing comes after you fall on your face a few times.

Your Kitchen Mindset

I'm always looking for ways I could do a job faster and more efficiently. Who has all day to spend in their kitchen? Why would you want to? As much as I love cooking, there are other things to do too.

My goal in the kitchen is to be fast and productive, but not rushed. I just want to be efficient at the task in front of me. That's what the next few chapters are for—finding practical ways to make this happen.

Chapter 24: The Holistic Household, Part 1: Eight Ways to Reduce Waste

Reducing waste is important to a frugal homestead. Waste means a piece isn't fitting—*connections are missing.* Here are several unconventional ways to reduce waste in your kitchen.

Eight Ways to Reduce Waste in the Kitchen

Think before you throw something in the trash. Many things people throw away can be reused. Here are eight ways you can reduce waste in your kitchen.

1. Fresh Vegetable Scraps—These can be saved in a gallon baggie in the freezer. Next time you make broth, throw them in your stockpot. Alternatively, put them in a bucket on the counter for your chickens or compost.

2. Rotten & Wilted Vegetables—If they are just a little wilted, cook them up in soups, or freeze them for the next time you make broth. Of course, you can feed them to your chickens or compost them.

> **Quick Tip**
> Collect bones, meat, and vegetable scraps in gallon freezer bags. Put in the bags anything you would throw in the stockpot. By keeping them in the freezer they are always ready and waiting, not molding in the fridge. Next time you make broth, pull the bag out of the freezer and add it to your pot.

3. Leftover Bones & Meat—After dinner, collect all the bone, meat, skin and fat scraps. Freeze them in a gallon resealable bag for making broth.

4. Paper Towels & Paper—If you use paper towels—no they're not a frugal invention for the homestead, but we use them—add the used ones to your compost. Printer paper and cardboard can be composted too. (I wouldn't compost them if there was a lot of printing on the paper or box.) Paper plates—that are really paper—can be composted. If they are coated in wax or plastic, I would throw them in the trash.

5. Old Milk—If it's raw milk that's soured or fermented—past the stage where you would want to drink it—feed it to the chickens or pigs. Alternatively, you can mix it in water and pour on your pasture. (Note: I wouldn't feed store-bought milk to our animals or put it on our pasture. When commercial milk goes bad it doesn't ferment and turn sour like raw milk; it rots and stinks.)

> "[Raw milk or whey]..is useful on both large areas or the smallest flowerpot with results that are consistently impressive. For years I had been congratulating myself on the exuberant growth of my rose bushes. I treated them with whey and milk washings and thought myself quite original, but no, some farmers have known this for years..David Wetzel..dressed sections of land with various ratios of raw skim milk or whey and water using a tractor-mounted spray rig. Results have been so gratifying that Wetzel urges those needing fertilizer to order up a tanker of milk from the nearest dairy. He suggests paying the farmer a premium over the meager price he would get from the co-op. 'It's worth more on the land,' he declares.
>
> Many formulations are possible, but according to Wetzel, a mixture of three gallons of milk to seventeen gallons of water is highly successful not only to promote vigorous growth of grass but to build lasting fertility." —*Keeping A Family Milk Cow* [1]

(For the small-scale homestead, that would be about 1 cup of milk or whey to every 6 cups of water.)

6. Over-Fermented Foods—Ferments can go wrong. Here are some things you can do to eliminate waste. Over-fermented kombucha can be fed to the chickens (it's like vinegar, so they won't drink a lot of it right away). Over-fermented kefir can be fed to them as well and they love it! Over-fermented sauerkraut and vegetables—as long as it's not moldy—can be fed to them, too. Apply these principles to other ferments gone old.

7. Broth & Leftovers—If the broth isn't moldy, only older than you would drink it—feed it to your chickens. Broth is good for them, they like it, and it's okay to feed it to them. If it's moldy, I'll sometimes dump it on the ground and let it soak in. (Make sure it all soaks in and dries up fairly quickly. If you live in a very moist climate, this may not be a good idea.)

Leftovers that are old—and not moldy—can be fed to the chickens. They'll eat about anything—chicken, beef, vegetables, fruit, casserole, soup, etc. Alternatively, compost all the vegetable and grain leftovers—mold and all. If the food has lots of meat, milk, or broth, don't compost it. They may cause problems in your compost pile.

Tip: When you feed broth, milk, or kefir to your chickens, give it to them in a bowl on a pallet to keep dirt out.

8. Grow the Right Foods—On the homestead it's easier to take a "trip to the garden" than a "trip to the store". Think about what you need and want to have on hand all the time, and then start growing these things.

Herbs are a great place to start. They're great in so many recipes, and growing them in your garden is handy. The fresh store-bought herbs come in tiny little boxes with a shelf life of a few days or less, and they can't compare in taste or smell with homegrown herbs.

Grow what your family already eats and loves. Experimenting is great after you get the basics down. Obviously, don't plant the foods your family hates or is allergic to.

Chapter 25: The Holistic Household, Part 2: System Efficiency

Homestead cooking needs to take *everything* into account. Stop wasting things that can be reused, and stop wasting time.

We're going to delve into system efficiency in the homestead kitchen. Let's look at system efficiency for food preparation, while cooking, and around the kitchen.

System Efficiency: Food Preparation

Start Dinner After Breakfast

If you start dinner in the morning, it's easily ready by dinner and there's only a tiny bit of work involved.

I use both the oven and slow-cooker, but I prefer the oven. The oven caramelizes and browns the chicken skin or outside of the roast, adding better flavor than the slow cooker does. I still use the slow-cooker every now and then though.

Tip: When cooking all day like this, I almost always take a roast right from the freezer without defrosting it. It's faster and I've been able to get consistent results (most of the time). It took a bit of trial and error when I started.

I'll take a medium size roast from the freezer and put it the oven at 350 degrees. I check it throughout the day and turn the temperature a little up or down depending on how it's doing and how long it is till dinner. It works.

I do this with a frozen whole chicken as well. Whole frozen chickens usually take less time so I start them a little later, cook them slower, and adjust however I need to time it right for dinner. Covering them is good and keeps moisture in.

> ### Technology Can Help
> Today, most people have a "smart phone". There are plenty of apps you can choose from to remind you to do things—like start dinner. When it's especially important for me to remember, I set an alarm on my phone—"Start a roast!!!".

Soaking Foods
Soaking beans, grains, nuts and seeds is easy. All you need to do is *remember*. It's fast to do, and it might take you five minutes. The health benefits are so great, and it is one of those extra steps you don't want to skip.

Set up a system or plan when you will soak beans. Maybe you would do it at night before bed or in the morning after breakfast. Get into a routine of soaking your foods.

> ### Soaking & Cooking Is Easy in the Instant Pot™
> Soaking—beans especially—is easy in the Instant Pot™ (a fancy crock pot pressure cooker). Soak the beans right in the pot, and leave it with the lid on till done. After soaking, strain off the water, dump them back in, and add in the ingredients needed. Plug it in. Turn it on. They are done in 40-50 minutes, and they always come out perfectly.

Fermenting
Fermented vegetables can be ready and waiting in the fridge. When it's dinner time, pull them out as a quick side dish that will go with any meal. The first thing I started fermenting was sauerkraut. Eventually my mom and dad always wanted me to make it, so I had to make it every time—*"Because you make it so well"*. *FYI that's how to get stuck with a chore!* After making it for a few years, I taught a younger sibling to make it. Now it's her chore.

Milk kefir is great made from fresh goat or cows milk. I make about a gallon a day and my five siblings and I drink it for breakfast. My ten-year-old brother, who milks the goats, also makes the kefir.

Pick a few favorites and stick with them. I'm more consistent making them when I do it every day (like our kefir) instead of one I have to do every so often.

System Efficiency: While Cooking

Plan Ahead & Always Be Ready

You need balance, and this isn't easy. Soak your grains and beans. Start a roast early in the morning. Be prepared, and then be ready for the days you forget, the times you can't and the surprises you don't expect.

Know how to go in the kitchen and whip up a quick meal. Frozen ground beef can be put in the pan and cooked up faster than you'd think, and lentils are a great bean that doesn't *have* to be soaked (although it's still better if they are). If I need a fast dinner, these are often options I choose.

I have days where I start dinner after breakfast, but other days I'm rushed to find and make something. I love to surprise our family with a yummy dinner, especially when they can't see what I could possibly make with what's in the house! It's a fun challenge to me. (My sister always says I make "something out of nothing," but I'm not sure about that.)

Learn a few things, get good at them, and then try a few more. Keep learning new ways and things to cook.

> ### Leveraging Cooking Heat to Your Advantage
> Save money by using your slow-cooker outside during the summer. You don't need an elaborate outdoor kitchen to cook outside. You can slow cook outside—all you need is a safe place where your animals can't get to it and a place to plug it in. You could even run an extension cord if needed. In winter, cook indoors to heat up the house—*see the connections!*

Cook With What You Have

This goes right along with what I was just talking about. Flexibility is important. If you aren't flexible now, as you get comfortable in the kitchen you'll be more open to experiment.

When cooking, if you don't have an ingredient, you have three options:
1. Go to the store and get it
2. Find a substitute
3. Skip it

1. **Go to the Store**—Plan out your shopping trips and go to the store as infrequently as possible. You don't want to be driving to the store everyday. Most homesteaders live too far away for that.
2. **Find a Substitute**—Many substitutes work just as well as the originally intended ingredient. Some are easier to make/use than others. There are lots of substitutes you can find online from things you may already have on hand.
3. **Skip It**—Many times you can skip the ingredient called for. Know what the ingredient does for the recipe—taste, texture, appearance, etc.—before skipping it. You may need to get a substitute or wait. For instance: you can't skip the eggs in your cookie recipe, or your cookie won't hold together. It won't be a cookie. If you're making chocolate chip cookies and don't have chocolate chips, you can skip them and still have a tasty cookie.

The Broth System

Broth helps with broken bones, digestive disorders, wounds, cancer, mental health and more! It's amazing for your health. Broth is easy to make and is made with: bones, meat, water, vegetables, herbs, salt, and vinegar. [1]

There are good and bad things to using either a stockpot or a slow cooker for your broth. I love how broth tastes from the stove! However, there's slightly more oversight needed. The smell and taste slow-cookers give the food isn't my favorite, but, they're convenient and easy to use.

The bones left after making broth can be reused. Reuse chicken bones once, and larger bones (beef, lamb, etc.) 3-4 or more times.

After making broth, even several times, you can still use the bones. If they're soft, and they will be if you reuse them, feed them to your dog, cat, chickens or pig. If you're careful, you may be able to compost them, but you may not want to do it too much. *(See page 44)* Since the fat has boiled out, they'll decompose faster. Get the most out of them by growing maggots for your chickens. They'll cut back on flies and provide food for chickens. *(See page 94)*

System Efficiency: Around the Kitchen

How to Make Your Own Systems

Finding an efficient system can be a challenge. Once you find one that works for you, it can save you time and money. It provides a peace of mind knowing that things are being cared for, stored, and used properly.

Often you don't realize you can do a better job because it can be hard to see. Try asking yourself questions:

> "Why do I _____ this way?"
> "Is there a better, more efficient way I could be doing _____?"

> *Fill in the blanks with: wash dishes, cook, organize, laundry, floors, windows, etc.*

If something isn't lining up, try something new. Find a new system, or come up with one. Be prepared to fail—failure is fine. Learn from your mistakes, and persevere in finding solutions to your problems. When a system works, stick with it.

Just because a system works well for one family, doesn't mean it will work well for yours. Keep this in mind as you figure out your systems. Every family is different, and everyone goes through different stages of life and has unique situations. You don't need to copy what everyone else is doing. Find the best systems for *your* family.

The following are two systems from our kitchen. Both made a huge difference in our kitchen efficiency.

Cup System—There are eight of us in our family. There's a problem when there are 39 cups on the counter every night!

There are many ideas on how you can help this problem. We tried a few systems, and they all failed.

Then mom came up with a great system. We have one counter for our family's cups. On the tile backsplash we have labels with our names. Each person's cup goes in front of their name. The older kids' cups are in the back and the younger ones in the front, so they can reach them easily. *(That was when we started this system. We're all older now.)*

Milk System—Since we've had goats, milk in the fridge is amazing! I love it. Soon after we got goats I found I had a new problem to deal with. We needed to keep the milk from going bad before we drank it. When siblings would go to the fridge, they'd get the newest milk, and eventually no-one wanted the oldest because it had soured.

The first part to milk system efficiency—switch to larger jars. Sixteen quart jars take more space than four one gallon jars. With lots of small jars, you lose them in the back of the fridge and they sour. **Ahem* Don't ask how.*

The second part of milk system efficiency—keep them together. If they're all in one place, you can with one quick look know what's what.

The third part of milk system efficiency—know how old each jar of milk is. This can be done in one of three ways.

1. Write the date on each jar.
2. Use magnets.[2]
3. Put away in a special order so you remember.

Write the Date on the Jars or Lids with a sharpie or dry erase marker. (The dry erase is easier to clean off.)

Use Magnets get or make a set of numbered magnets (1, 2, 3, etc.) and put them on the lids. "One" is the oldest and the highest number is the newest. (This only works with metal lids.)

Put Away in a Special Order So You Remember. This one is my favorite. No sharpie to clean off jars, and most of my lids are plastic. On a shelf in the fridge, find a place you can dedicate to the milk. Take a piece of masking tape and place it the length you think your milk will take. Write on it, "Newest -- Use the Oldest first! ---> Oldest". Always place the newest milk where it goes and as you use up the oldest milk, slide up the newer. This has saved me tons of time, and "losing milk" is way less of a problem.

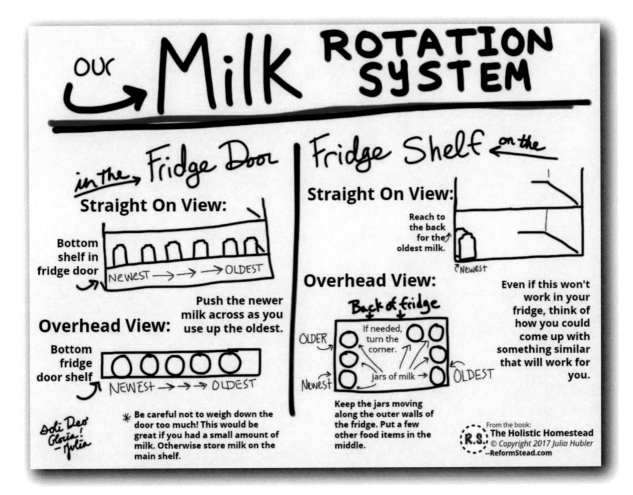

Chapter 26: The Holistic Household, Part 3: Preserving & a Few Projects

Two things a homesteader is going to be doing are preserving and projects. Let's take a holistic look.

Preserving Methods:

Canning

There are two kinds of canning—water bath and pressure. Between the two you can preserve almost any food.

Canning Pros:
- Canned food needs no electricity or power to keep for a long time.
- Almost everything can be canned!
- Lots of people do it, so there are lots of recipes to get you started.

Canning Cons:
- Lots of upfront work.
- Costs more than some other preserving methods, if you need to purchase the jars, canner, produce, etc.
- Canned food doesn't have the health benefits found in fermented foods.
- Some folks say the canning process harms the food, and others say the opposite. You'll need to research and decide.

Water Bath Versus Pressure Canning—If you want to can more than a few things, you'll need to learn both. Water bath canning is best for high-acid foods such as tomatoes, jams, etc. Pressure canning is the *only safe* canning option for low acid foods like beans, meat, etc. *(See the Resources Chapter for my favorite canning instructional DVD.)*

Fermenting

Fermenting can be used as a way to store your food. It adds healthy bacteria to the food that's good for you.

Fermenting Pros:
- Makes food last longer.
- Adds many healthy probiotics—great for your health.
- You can ferment pretty much anything!

Fermenting Cons:
- Some ferments don't last long at room temperature. They may need refrigeration. (Or store in a root cellar—if you have one.)
- Be careful! If you have a histamine intolerance, you may not be able to handle ferments. In that case, fermenting won't be a good option. (Few people do—only about 1%.)

Tips for Long-Term Storage—Most fermented recipes I find say the ferment has a short out-of-the-fridge shelf life. They'll get too fermented if left out too long. Sauerkraut is the only exception I know of.

A cool cellar or basement was the typical storage place from fall to spring for many traditional ferments. (Even in Arizona!) Storing them down there extends their shelf life.

Dehydrating

I love dehydrating foods because it's a great way to use the sunshine. I also love the ease of packing and storing the light food.

Dehydrating Pros:
- It can be cheap—sunshine is free, but electric dehydrators cost money to run.
- Dehydrated foods are light and easy to carry, store and use.
- Dehydrated foods are great for taking on trips, camping, or hiking.
- Dehydrated foods are easily rehydrated in water.

- You can throw dehydrated vegetables in soup.

Dehydrating Cons:
- Wet, rainy areas may not be idea for solar dehydrating. However, electric dehydrating is an option in this situation.

Electric Dehydrating—Dehydrating with an electric dehydrator is easy. Buy one and start using it.

I like to use both our electric dehydrator and the sun. The indoor dehydrator is easier for small quantities of food, and dehydrating outdoors gives you more space for larger quantities of food.

Solar Dehydrating—Dehydrating foods right in the sunshine is one of my favorite preserving methods! Here in Arizona, there's no reason not to take advantage of all the sunshine. All you need is a clean place. Here are a few different options. (In all of the following methods, keep the food safe and away from animals.)

Example: drying on a line. These two t-posts give us lots of space to dry our citrus peels and other vegetables.

Sun Dehydrating Method #1. String them up. Unfortunately, not all things work for this. For the ones that can, this is easy and takes little space.

Sun Dehydrating Method #2. On a cookie sheet, tray, screen, cloth or sheet.

"On the clean grass Ma spread clean cloths, and Laura and Mary laid the plums on the cloths, to dry in the sun." —*On The Banks Of Plum Creek, by Laura Ingalls Wilder* [1]

Fun Dehydrating Ideas

Dehydrated Cherry Tomato Halves Cut them in half and dehydrate. They're amazing plain or in soups, rice, chili, etc.

Banana Sticks Peel a banana and cut in half width-wise. Push your finger in the center of the cut you just made. The banana will split into three "sticks". Dehydrate them and eat as yummy snacks.

Portable Broth Boil broth down as thick as you can. When it's a thick gel, dehydrate on solid trays. When it's brittle, break it into pieces and take it with you on trips. Rehydrate in hot water.

Citrus Vitamin C Dehydrate citrus peels, and blend or grind them in a food processor. Strain them for a finer powder, that you can use for yourself or animals. Vitamin C made out of real food like this is more readily absorbed in the bodies of people and animals.

Freezing

My favorite things to freeze are small, take up little space, and make a big difference to the meal. Chopped or sliced tomatoes and chopped onions take little room and can make a plain meal yummy. (I like to add those two to lentils and chili.) You can add them to a soup while they're still frozen.

Freezing Pros:
- Easy prep work
- Low initial input
- Easy to use

Freezing Cons:
- Freezing takes a lot of space.
- You *need electricity* to keep everything frozen.

Preserving Comparison Chart:

Method	Skill Level	Shelf Life	Start Up Costs	Notes:
Canning—Waterbath	Intermediate	Long	High	For both types of canning you'll need to buy: lids, rings and jars.
Canning—Pressure	Intermediate	Long	Very High	These canners can get expensive.
Fermenting	Beginner	Varies	Low-High	The health benefits to this are amazing!
Dehydrating—Sun	Beginner	Long	Low-None	Sunshine is free!
Dehydrating—Electric	Beginner	Long	Low-High	Price varies depending on the dehydrator you buy.
Freezing	Beginner	Varies*	Low-High	You need power to keep a freezer going.

*The amount of time varies widely based upon the food and how it was packaged.

Three Indoor Projects/Crafts

1. Recycled Rags

A great way to use old T-shirts, non-reparable clothing (heavy duty woven fabric like jeans, canvas, etc.) and knit fabric is to cut it apart and turn it into rags. Knit fabric has an advantage because it doesn't unravel and there's no need to hem the edges.

How do you do it? Cut your fabric or t-shirts into squares or rectangles. I recommend having a few standard sizes and sort them according to size. Then when you go for one, you can grab the size you need instead of looking for the right one. Try a large, medium and/or small.

You can use these rags for udder washing, around the house or outside, and/or instead of paper towels.

2. DIY Lip Balm Recipe: In Three Easy Steps

I've been making and selling this lip balm for the last few years at our local homeschool convention. Every year I've had people come back, tell me they like it, and stock up for next year. Seeing how many people loved it I thought I would include the recipe. It's easy to make.

You'll Need:
2 tablespoons grated beeswax, tightly packed
2 tablespoons shea butter
2 teaspoons avocado or olive oil
Optional: 10-30 drops of your favorite essential oil*

- Step #1. In a double boiler (or a pot with a bowl in it), melt together beeswax, shea butter, and avocado oil.
- Step #2. Once they're melted all the way, take off the heat and add in your desired essential oils. Mix it together.
- Step #3. Pour into your lip balm containers and let sit until cool.

*There are more flavor options and ideas on my website. [2]

Easy No-Spill Tip:

Use a rubber band to hold the lip balm tubes together. Keeping them together makes them harder to tip over—*which happens.*

3. Practical & Pretty in the Kitchen

I love it when you can take something useful and make it beautiful too! One thing I've

done in the kitchen is take the Costco plasticware boxes and cover them with paper that goes with our kitchen. We use the plastic forks and spoons when we have people over, so they're important, but we don't need to pull them out every day.

To do it, all you need is pretty paper that goes with your kitchen. Tape or glue the paper to the outside of the boxes, then "paint" the whole outside of the box with Mod Podge®. Now you can store them as part of your kitchen's decor above the cabinets.

You can also use matching paper to cover the edges of a marker board in the kitchen. Follow the same procedure as with the boxes: glue on the paper, then "paint" on the Mod Podge®.

Chapter 27: The Holistic Household, Part 4: Family Health

You're growing all those herbs and garlic. Don't forget they're good for your health as well. Herbs do two things: they support health and are healing when you're sick.

Health Supporting—Add herbs to your food. They do more than make a meal taste appetizing because they have other beneficial functions.

> "Though we tend to associate the flavor of certain herbs with certain foods — basil with tomatoes, cloves with meat, horseradish with hearty meat dishes — often these pairings came about for medicinal reasons, not flavor. Basil aids with the digestion of the acids in tomatoes; cloves and other spices helped preserve meat in prerefrigeration days; and horseradish stimulates sluggish digestion and aids in the digestion of fatty foods."
>
> —*Rosemary Gladstar's Medicinal Herbs—A Beginner's Guide* [1]

Healing—Herbs are also great for fighting sicknesses. There are so many herbs and they help with thousands of illnesses. You could spend your whole life studying them.

The good thing is you don't need to. Learn what a few of the basic ones are for and use them often when you need them. You need to have a good herbal remedies book on hand for looking things up. *(See the Resources Chapter, page 192)*

My Five Favorite Natural Health Boosters

1. Garlic is a big one. It's antibacterial and antiviral and is good for just about everything.

2. Cayenne is great for coughs and sore throats. Mix it with apple cider vinegar and gargle with it. (I hope you like spicy! *Ouch! Not me!*)

3. Apple cider vinegar is great for the immune system, contains probiotics, is an energy booster, improves digestion, and is good for aches and sprains. It's high in lots of minerals, including potassium.

4. Fresh ginger tea is great for colds, the flu, and an upset stomach.

5. Chamomile tea is great to help you sleep at night.

---> Part 4 <---

Put the Pieces Together!

Chapter 28: The Holistic Homestead

Can you make the connections yet? Are you fitting the pieces together? I hope so. The purpose of this book is for *you* to be able to make practical connections on your homestead.

Start homesteading with the right mindset. Have an overarching plan and goal. You want an organized system, not a bunch of disjoined parts and pieces.

When the pieces of a car are put together correctly, the car runs smoothly. When there's a problem with *one* of the important pieces, the whole car is dysfunctional. You need a homestead "car" that more than functions—one that runs *smoothly.*

The Right Mindset

Don't be afraid to fail. Sometimes that's what it takes. It's better to fail, than to not try at all. You need a love for the learning process.

Set a goal and make a plan. When you know where you're headed, everything in between lines up better.

I've included as many connections as I can, but there are so many more. I've shown you how lots of the pieces can fit together, but now it's your turn.

You now know how to use all the "How-To" homesteading books. You can look at all the projects and know how they fit—or not—on your homestead.

No goal = aimless work. When you have your goal, you're ready to start!

Get outside and take action. You know what you're aiming for, you've got your sights on the target, and now all you need to do is shoot. It's easy!

"You just do it!" [1]

Take It in Steps

Don't get overwhelmed! Homesteading is a process, and you can't do overnight. You won't make a one-eighty in one day. When it comes down to getting things done on your homestead—just take it one step at a time.

Final Words

It's up to you now. It's time for me to leave, and let you make connections. Look, see, and put the pieces together on *your* homestead.

In wrapping up, I hope you've learned a lot. I know writing this has shown me much. One thing it taught me is it takes a lot of work and perseverance to write a book! It's also helped me see better and hone in on my philosophy of homesteading.

I haven't got it all down yet. I'm still learning. It's work, and I enjoy it.

Holistic homesteading is taking dominion of Christ's earth and bringing all things under His feet. *It's Kingdom advancing work!*

Soli Deo Gloria! *(Glory Be to God Alone!)*

"For as the earth brings forth its bud, as the garden causes the
things that are sown in it to spring forth,
So the Lord GOD will cause righteousness and praise to spring forth
before all the nations."
—*Isaiah 61:11 (NKJV)*

Resources & Notes—*How & Where to Learn More*

It's always sad when you get to the end of a good educational book, and don't know where you can keep learning more great information along the same lines of what you just read. *Where do you go now? How do you find more good material to read and further your research?*

This may be one of the most **valuable** sections in this book. Reading *one book* won't give you all the answers you need to run a successful homestead. You need to read, study, and read some more. This is how you can learn and grow your homestead with *fewer* mistakes.

The books that are full of *words* and not much practical information—*they drive me crazy!* I hate wasting my time *(and money if I bought it)* with them! When someone takes two chapters to say what could have been said in two paragraphs—that's a waste of my time. I want to read lots of *amazing* books that are *jam-packed* with **helpful information. This is why this section is so important!** ALL of my recommendations are *only* the absolute **best** of what I've read, learned and found on the given subjects.

Besides reading websites, studying books and watching educational DVDs—I have learned lots of the great info and tips that are throughout this book from friends. Look at what others are doing and learn from their successes and failures. You can learn *so much* this way!

Just so you know—I do not agree with *everything* in many of the resources and books I recommend. Especially some of their unbiblical religious presuppositions. Yet in all of them, I found something especially *valuable* and important you can learn and apply to your homestead.

The ones marked with an asterisk* I especially like for their open stance on Christianity.

Happy learning!—*Soli Deo Gloria!*

The Holistic-Permaculture-Homestead Book & Resources List—*The Places I Look First*

General Holistic Books & Resources:
Books: *You Can Farm*, **and other books by Joel Salatin*** Each book I've read by Salatin has always been a fun, interesting and informative read! He takes holistic and permaculture principles and applies them to farming. Lots of great info for homesteaders.

Books: The *Storey's* **Homesteading Books, by Various Authors** The time-proven Storey's books are loved by many homesteaders. They are known to be helpful and very practical. I especially like the one we have about goats, when the authors (Belanger & Bredesen) share how you can keep goats on pasture.

Great info, extremely valuable, and good to have on-hand—yet often they are a bit more conventional on some topics than I'd like.

Book: *Practical Permaculture*, by Jessi Bloom and Dave Boehnlein Lots of helpful holistic information. Very, as it says, *practical*.

Website: *ThePrairieHomestead.com*, by Jill Winger* A great homesteading blog full of helpful articles and valuable content—on a nice, easy-to-navigate site. If I'm looking something up—I try to find it here or at the following blog…

Website: *ReformationAcres.com*, by Quinn* Another favorite homestead blog. Again, good articles and content—on a beautiful user-friendly website.

Gardening, Orchard, Rain & Greywater Books & Resources:

Book: *Teeming with Microbes*, by Lowenfels and Lewis A foundational must-have! This book shows how microbes work and shows you how to have a truly natural, or better than organic—garden, pasture and orchard.

Book: *The Holistic Orchard*, by Michael Phillips A wonderful book, full of natural, permaculture and holistic practices for fruit trees and orchards. The info in this book fits perfectly with the microbial awareness demonstrated in *Teeming with Microbes.* Jam-packed with practical, helpful information—perfect for the homestead.

Books: Gardening, local Finding a good gardening book for your area is a good plan—especially if you live in a desert, like Phoenix AZ. Two books I recommend if you live in the desert: ***Extreme Gardening,* by Dave Owens**, and ***Desert Gardening,* by Brookbank.** Both have valuable info for the desert's unique challenges. If you live elsewhere, look up or ask around and find a good gardening book for your climate.

Book: *Perennial Vegetables*, by Eric Toensmeier If perennial vegetables are a consideration, this book has lots of information about many different kinds you can try. A good starting book if you're interested in perennial vegetables.

Book: *Seed to Seed*, by Suzanne Ashworth If you want to start saving seeds this book gives you great, *in-depth* advice.

Website: *RareSeeds.com*, Baker Creek Heirloom Seeds Company* I love this seed company and have purchased most of my seeds from them.

Book: *Create An Oasis With Greywater*, by Art Ludwig A comprehensive, practical, how-to guide. A great book if you want to start turning your greywater into water for shade trees and fruit trees.

Book: *Rainwater Harvesting for Drylands and Beyond*, by Brad Lancaster Great info for anyone who wants to harvest rainwater. There are a few volumes to this book. It is very practical, and has lots of black and white pictures to show you lots of the different rainwater harvesting methods.

Chickens & Fowl Books & Resources:

Book: *The Small-Scale Poultry Flock*, **by Harvey Ussery** If you could only buy *one* book about chickens—look no further. This is by far the *best* I've seen. Full of everything you need to know about chickens and other domesticated fowls—very practical. *(The Foreword is by Joel Salatin.)*

Website: *AbundantPermaculture.com*, **by Justin Rhodes** Known as the, "permaculture chickens guy" Justin Rhodes has an lots of extremely valuable information about how to raise chickens—all from a holistic, permaculture based mindset. He is also branching out into other homestead topics besides chickens. Very down-to-earth, practical, and ***valuable*** information! I highly recommend checking out his website, articles and videos.

Website: The *Sustainable Poultry Network (SPN),* **http://spnusa.com** A great place to try to locate a good heritage chicken or fowl breeder near you.

Milk Cows & Goats Books & Resources:

Website: *MistyMorningFarmVA.com*, **by Faith & Adam S.*** If you want valuable, holistic information on milk cows—head on over to their site. I love all of their information I've read/heard so far!!! They're super nice and very helpful.

Book: *Keeping A Family Cow*, **by Joann S. Grohman** A great book to have on-hand if you own a milk cow —or plan to in the future.

Book: *Devil In The Milk*, **by Keith Woodford** If you want to learn more about A1 and A2 genetics, this is the book to read. I haven't read the whole thing, but what I have read is very informative. This is considered *the* book on A1 and A2 genetics in cows and how it affects proteins their milk—and therefore you, the consumer.

Kitchen, Healthy Food & Preserving Books & Resources:

Books: *Nourishing Traditions & Nourishing Broth*, **by Sally Fallon (Morell)** If there was just one cookbook I had to pick it would be *Nourishing Traditions.* Packed with tons of informative, helpful, practical, cooking and food preparation advice and recipes. *Nourishing Broth* (By Sally Fallon Morell and Kaayla Daniel) is also loaded with information—if you want to learn more about broth.

E-book: *Cheesemaking Made Easy*, **by Dina-Marie** This *ebook* is great if you want to start making cheese. It's full of lots of yummy recipes, mozzarella, cheddar, cultured butter, kefir and more. I especially *love* the mozzarella recipe!

DVD: *At Home Canning For Beginners & Beyond*, **by Kendra Lynne** If you thought canning was hard or scary—no longer! In this DVD, as Kendra takes you into her kitchen, she shows you just how simple water bath and pressure canning really are. *A confidence-building DVD.*

Herbal & Natural Health Books & Resources:

Book: *Rosemary Gladstar's Medicinal Herbs: A Beginner's Guide*, **by Rosemary Gladstar** A wonderful book to get you started with using herbs for your family. Beautiful full-color pictures and easy to use.

Book: *Rosemary Gladstar's Herbal Recipes For Vibrant Health*, by Rosemary Gladstar Another good reference book. Includes 175 recipes and remedies. Very user-friendly.

Find All These Resources & More on My Website for Easy Reference

ReformStead.com/homestead_resources.html

Notes From the Book:

Chapter 3: Six Pivotal Points To Starting A Successful Homestead
1. Salatin, J. (1998). *You Can Farm.* pp. 61
2. Salatin, J. (1998). *You Can Farm.* pp. 61
3. Salatin, J. (1998). *You Can Farm.* pp. 61

Chapter 4: Grass Is Key!
1. *The Horse Your Guide To Equine Health Care.* (2010, September 1). Retrieved June 28, 2017, from http://www.thehorse.com/articles/26829/multi-species-grazing-horses-and-cows-and-goats-oh-my
2. Grohman, J. S. (2013). *Keeping A Family Cow.* pp. 196-7
3. *The Horse Your Guide To Equine Health Care.* (2010, September 1). Retrieved June 28, 2017, from http://www.thehorse.com/articles/26829/multi-species-grazing-horses-and-cows-and-goats-oh-my

Chapter 5: The Microbial Conscious Gardener
1. Lowenfels, J. and Lewis, W. (2014). *Teaming With Microbes.*
2. Lowenfels, J. and Lewis, W. (2014). *Teaming With Microbes.* pp. 43
3. Lowenfels, J. and Lewis, W. (2014). *Teaming With Microbes.* pp. 147

Chapter 7: The Orchard & Fruit Tree Guilds
1. Phillips, M. (2011). *The Holistic Orchard.* pp. 108

Chapter 8: Holistic Vegetable Gardening
1. *Baker Creek,* is where I've gotten most of my seeds, and they've been great! http://www.rareseeds.com/
2. I've found, *Seed To Seed,* by Suzanne Ashworth, a great resource.

Chapter 10: Weeds—A Problem or Temporary Solution?
1. Phillips, M. (2011). *The Holistic Orchard.* pp. 32-33
2. Lowenfels, J. and Lewis, W. (2014). *Teaming With Microbes.* pp. 194

Chapter 11: Beneficial Insects & Holistic Pest Control
1. Phillips, M. (2011). *The Holistic Orchard.* pp. 122
2. Lowenfels, J. and Lewis, W. (2014). *Teaming With Microbes.* pp. 195-196

Chapter 12: Rainwater & Greywater On The Homestead
1. Ludwig, A. (2015). *Create An Oasis With Greywater, 6th edition.* pp. 18
2. Ludwig, A. (2015). *Create An Oasis With Greywater, 6th edition.* pp. 2 & 18

Chapter 13: Holistic Chickens
1. The *Sustainable Poultry Network (SPN)* is the best place to start! http://spnusa.com/ | If there is nothing there, check out the *livestock conservancy.* http://livestockconservancy.org/index.php/heritage

Chapter 14: Beyond Chickens—Guineas, Ducks & More
1. Phillips, M. (2011). *The Holistic Orchard.* pp. 117

2. Ussery, H. (2011). *The Small-Scale Poultry Flock.* pp. 228

Chapter 15: Milk Cows & Goats, Part 1: Which Is Best For You?
1. Salatin, J. (1998). *You Can Farm.*
2. Wilder, L. (1994). *Farmer Boy.* pp. 241

Chapter 16: Milk Cows & Goats, Part 2: Two Important Considerations
1. Woodford, K. (2009). *Devil In The Milk.* pp. 37
2. Woodford, K. (2009). *Devil In The Milk.* pp. 37
3. Woodford, K. (2009). *Devil In The Milk.*
4. MistyMorningFarmVA.com
5. **Here are several places you can start researching this:** http://www.motherearthnews.com/homesteading-and-livestock/raising-cattle/small-breed-milk-cows | http://mistymorningfarmva.com/what-do-we-mean-by-grazing-genetics-2/ | MistyMorningFarmVA.com
6. Fallon, S. with Enig, M. G. Ph.D. (2001). *Nourishing Traditions.* pp. 88
7. *Misty Morning Farm.* (2011, October 24). Retrieved June 28, 2017, from http://mistymorningfarmva.com/why-do-we-raise-our-calves-on-real-milk/
8. *Wikipedia The Free Encyclopedia.* (2017, May 28) Retrieved June 28, 2017, from https://en.wikipedia.org/wiki/Dairy_cattle
9. MistyMorningFarmVA.com

Chapter 18: Keeping Roosters, Bucks, Rams & Bulls
1. Thanks to Mrs. Ronsick *(my friend & editor)* for the info on rams.
2. Thanks to Faith from *MistyMorningFarmVA.com,* for the info on the bulls.

Chapter 19: Natural Remedies & Animal Health On The Homestead
1. Belanger, J. and Bredesen, S. (2010). *Storey's Guide to Raising Dairy Goats.*
2. High Energy Blend, from *Lancaster Agg,* http://www.lancasterag.com/HomePage
3. If you want to get a feeding syringe, I found mine at *Jeffers,* https://www.jefferspet.com/
4. Grohman, J. S. (2013). *Keeping A Family Cow.* pp. 175-6

Chapter 20: Fly Control & Prevention
1. Salatin, J. (1998). *You Can Farm.*
2. I found directions at *ThePrairieHomestead.com,* for a natural DIY fly trap.

Chapter 21: Holistic Points Applied
1. York, A. (1998). *Sergeant York and The Great War (edited by Richard Wheeler).* pp. 42

Chapter 24: The Holistic Household, Part 1: 8 Ways To Reduce Waste
1. Grohman, J. S. (2013). *Keeping a Family Cow.* pp. 193-4

Chapter 25: The Holistic Household, Part 2: System Efficiency
1. Good info on broth can be found in this book: Morell, S. F. and Daniel, K. T. PhD, CCN. (2014). *Nourishing Broth.*
2. Thanks to Mrs. Ronsick for this great idea!

Chapter 26: The Holistic Household, Part 3: Preserving & A Few Projects
1. Wilder, L. (1994). *On The Banks Of Plum Creek.* pp. 63
2. ReformStead.com

Chapter 27: The Holistic Household, Part 4: Family Health
1. Gladstar R. (2012). *Rosemary Gladstar's Medicinal Herbs A Beginners Guide.* pp. 50

Chapter 28: The Holistic Homestead
1. Salatin, J. (1998). *You Can Farm.* pp. 61

Appendix

How to use the appendix: I've included the charts found throughout the book back here in one place. One reason is so they're easier to see and read. The other is so you can find them all in one place. They are listed here in the order they appear in the book. The table of contents below is for quick reference.

Appendix Index:

How-To Make CONNECTIONS

to your homestead

THE 3 "RULES":

1. There should be ZERO waste.

2. Everything needs to be CONNECTED to something else on your homestead. Nothing should function in isolation.

3. Other parts of your homestead need to BENEFIT from it. How can it HELP & SERVE your homestead?

ask → Why? NOT
→ Do I need a better system?
→ Is it the wrong time?
→ Do I live in the wrong climate?
→ Why isn't it working?

Soli Deo Gloria! —Julia

From the book:
The Holistic Homestead
© Copyright 2017 Julia Hubler
--ReformStead.com
R.S.

Whichever part of your homestead you're evaluating, it should meet the 3 "rules". If not, reconsider. See if you can adjust and make it work or if it's better to pitch the idea altogether.

If something does not line up with the 3 "rules", start asking questions. Try to find out *why* it isn't working.

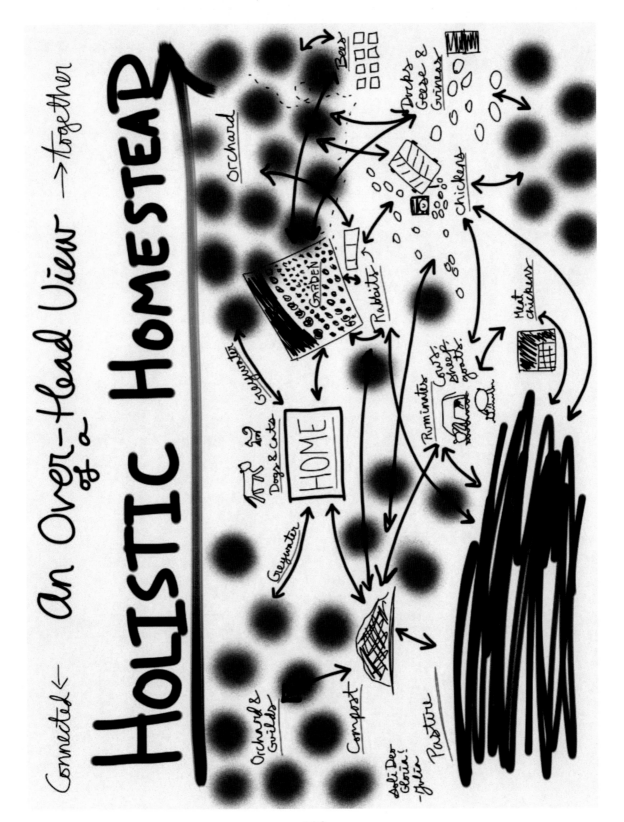

Connected ← An Over-Head View of a →together

HOLISTIC HOMESTEAD

Orchard

Bees

Ducks, Geese & Guineas

Chickens

Garden

Rabbits

Meat Chickens

Greywater

Ruminants
Cows, sheep, goats.

Dogs & Cats

HOME

Greywater

Orchard & Guilds

Compost

Pasture

Soli Deo Gloria! —Julia

Grass & Your Animals

Three things are important for healthy pasture & animals: Multiple species of ruminants, rotational grazing & chickens.

Cows, goats, and sheep like to eat different herbage. This diverse taste is part of the reason a combination of animals is more efficient. More of your pasture will be eaten.

Cows eat grass differently than sheep (goats prefer weeds). Sheep bite the grass off with their teeth. Cows, on the other hand, wrap their tongue around the longer grass, rip it, and then chew and eat it.

Parasites on pasture are reduced when you rotate diffrent animals on pasture--one after the other.

More animals can fit on the same amount of pasture with several species.

Animals that are pasture raised are themselves healthier.

Their milk--or meat when butchered--is healthier for you to drink or eat. There is less of the bad fats and more of the good ones like omega 3.

Rotating improves pasture. Manure & grazing are spread over ALL of your grass instead of only in their "favorite spots".

Chickens are great on the pasture. They're good for the grass and the animals' health. They spread the manure and eat out of it the bad bugs, parasites and flies.

From the book:
R.S. The Holistic Homestead
© Copyright 2017 Julia Hubler
--ReformStead.com

200

Compost & Your Homestead

Compost completes the circles to many parts of the homestead.

Compost Pile

The compost pile is a great place to throw your kitchen scraps.

Compost manure from animal pens. This keeps their living envionment cleaner.

Spread compost on your grass to improve your pasture and grow more and better food for your animals.

You can't have too much compost. Make as much as you can and use it everywhere!

Compost is a source of chicken food (bugs, larvae, etc.) and a place for them to work.

Compost supplies the garden with organic matter.

Compost gives all of your soil a great microbial boost.

Soli Deo Gloria! —Julia

From the book:
The Holistic Homestead
© Copyright 2017 Julia Hubler
--ReformStead.com
R.S.

Bird's-eye View of a... Guild
Permaculture

As the center tree grows, its canopy shades and protects the whole guild.

Blackberries & grapes, etc. VINES

Deep-rooted Comfrey

Mix Them Up! Spread a diversity of plants around the base of your center tree.

Center TREE

Herbs

Ground cover like clover or buckwheat. Blackberries & grapes, etc. VINES

Larger herb: rosemary

Herbs

Keep 2-3 inches of fungal mulch over the soil.

Spreading herbs: thyme, mint, etc.

Small tree or shrub

Deep-rooted, mineral mining plants

Beneficial insects & honey bees

VINES

A small tree: like a pomegranate or fig

Or a nitrogen fixing plant

Or a native plant

Herbs

Soli Deo Gloria! –Julia

From the book:
The Holistic Homestead
© Copyright 2017 Julia Hubler
--ReformStead.com
R.S.

Permaculture Guild — CHOOSING THE CENTER Tree

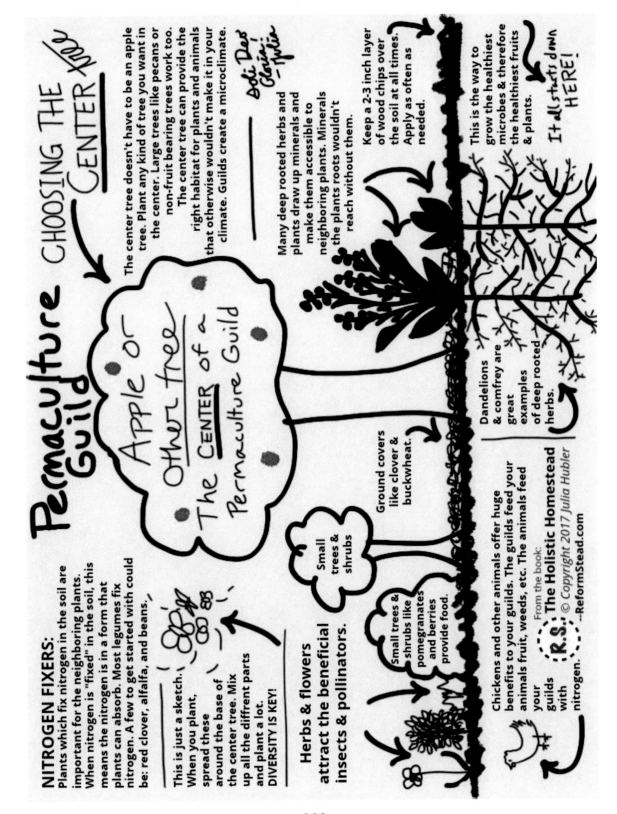

Apple or Other Tree

The CENTER of a Permaculture Guild

The center tree doesn't have to be an apple tree. Plant any kind of tree you want in the center. Large trees like pecans or non-fruit bearing trees work too. The center tree can provide the right habitat for plants and animals that otherwise wouldn't make it in your climate. Guilds create a microclimate.

Soli Deo Gloria! —Julia

Many deep rooted herbs and plants draw up minerals and make them accessible to neighboring plants. Minerals the plants roots wouldn't reach without them.

Keep a 2-3 inch layer of wood chips over the soil at all times. Apply as often as needed.

This is the way to grow the healthiest microbes & therefore the healthiest fruits & plants.

It all starts down HERE!

Dandelions & comfrey are great examples of deep rooted herbs.

NITROGEN FIXERS:
Plants which fix nitrogen in the soil are important for the neighboring plants. When nitrogen is "fixed" in the soil, this means the nitrogen is in a form that plants can absorb. Most legumes fix nitrogen. A few to get started with could be: red clover, alfalfa, and beans.

This is just a sketch. When you plant, spread these around the base of the center tree. Mix up all the diffrent parts and plant a lot. DIVERSITY IS KEY!

Herbs & flowers attract the beneficial insects & pollinators.

Small trees & shrubs

Small trees & shrubs like pomegranates and berries provide food.

Ground covers like clover & buckwheat.

Chickens and other animals offer huge benefits to your guilds. The guilds feed your animals fruit, weeds, etc. The animals feed your guilds with nitrogen.

From the book:
The Holistic Homestead
© Copyright 2017 Julia Hubler
—ReformStead.com

Guild Example

#1.
From our backyard

Things To Do
- Herbs
- Flowers
- Nitrogen Fixers
- Ground Covers

Deep taprooted plants

Deep taprooted plants

Deep taprooted plants

Center APPLE Tree

Deep taprooted plants

Wood Chip -Mulch-

Small pomegranate

Plants with a deep taproot (dandelions, comfrey, etc.)

The green in these charts is the leaves and shade the tree's canopy provides the guild once established.

Chickens can come and eat the bugs and fertilize.

Soli Deo Gloria! —Julia

From the book:
R.S. The Holistic Homestead
© Copyright 2017 Julia Hubler
--ReformStead.com

Guild Example

#2.

From our backyard

Things TBD
- Small Tree or Shrub
- Flowers
- Nitrogen Fixer
- Ground Cover

Herbs:
Rosemary
Sage
Thyme

Deep taprooted plants

Black Berry VINE

Wood Chips -Mulch-

Center FIG Tree

Deep taprooted plants

Deep taprooted plants

Purple sweet potatoes

Guineas roam around, eat the bugs and fertilize.

Soli Deo Gloria! —Julia

From the book:
The Holistic Homestead
© Copyright 2017 Julia Hubler
--ReformStead.com

R.S.

Guild Example #3.

From our backyard

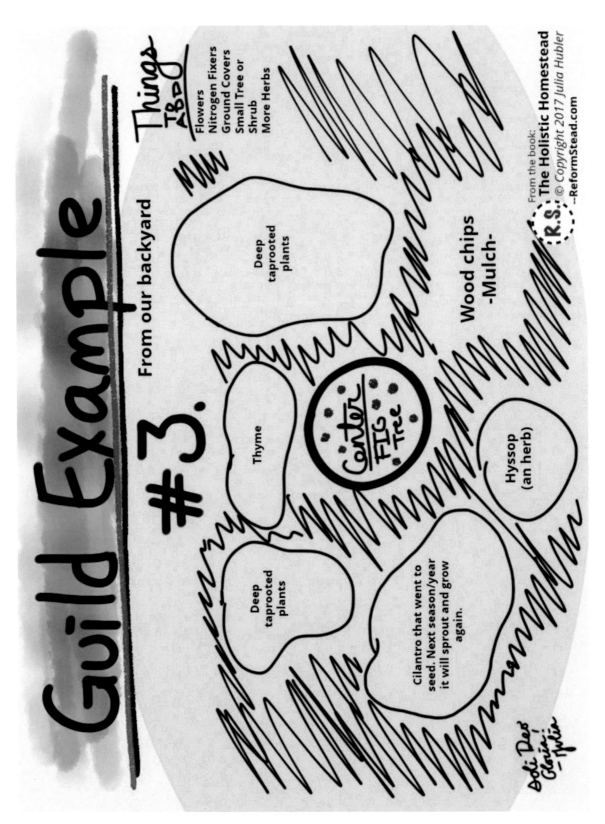

Things TBD
Flowers
Nitrogen Fixers
Ground Covers
Small Tree or Shrub
More Herbs

Deep taprooted plants

Thyme

Center FIG Tree

Hyssop (an herb)

Deep taprooted plants

Cilantro that went to seed. Next season/year it will sprout and grow again.

Wood chips -Mulch-

From the book:
R.S. The Holistic Homestead
© Copyright 2017 Julia Hubler
--ReformStead.com

Soli Deo Gloria! --Julia

Guild Example

#4.

From our backyard

Things To Add
Herbs
Flowers
Nitrogen Fixers
Ground Covers

Chickens are on patrol for the bugs and fertilize while they're at it.

Deep taprooted plant

Center APRICOT Tree

Pomegranate

Wood Chips -Mulch-

Creosote

Deep taprooted plant

Soli Deo Gloria! —Julia

From the book:
The Holistic Homestead
R.S.
© Copyright 2017 Julia Hubler
--ReformStead.com

Corn, Squash & Beans

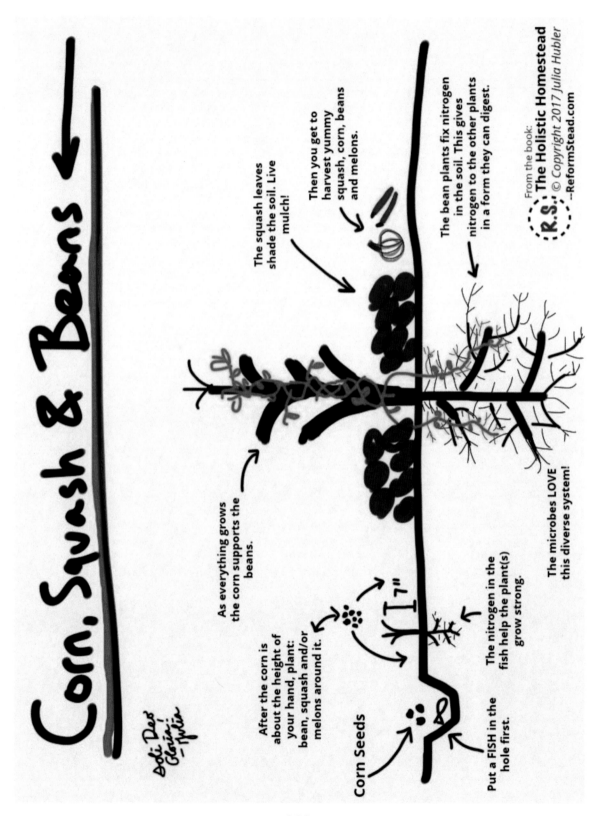

Soli Deo Gloria! —Julia

As everything grows the corn supports the beans.

The squash leaves shade the soil. Live mulch!

Then you get to harvest yummy squash, corn, beans and melons.

The bean plants fix nitrogen in the soil. This gives nitrogen to the other plants in a form they can digest.

After the corn is about the height of your hand, plant: bean, squash and/or melons around it.

Corn Seeds

7"

The nitrogen in the fish help the plant(s) grow strong.

Put a FISH in the hole first.

The microbes LOVE this diverse system!

From the book:
R.S. The Holistic Homestead
© Copyright 2017 Julia Hubler
--ReformStead.com

Two Planting Methods →Compared

Uneven Pattern

Notice, when the plants are "slightly squeezed" together more fit in less space.

Another option is to plant in a square grid.

Smaller plants get smaller squares.

Larger squares for larger plants.

These plants are "slightly squeezed" - not packed. You still need to thin and keep space between them.

From the book:
The Holistic Homestead
R.S. © Copyright 2017 Julia Hubler
---ReformStead.com

Straight Rows

See all the wasted space between and in the rows?

Cabbage

Beets

Lettuce

Soli Deo Gloria! —Julia

How to Protect a new tree from chickens.

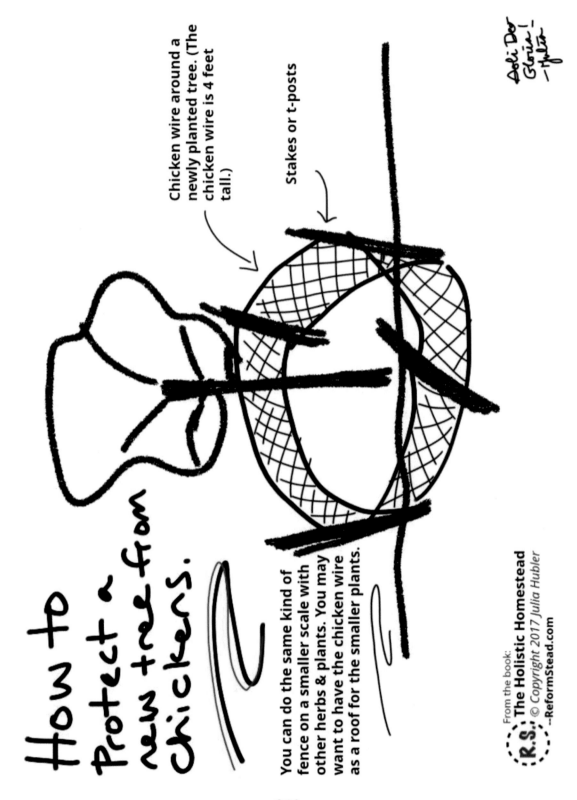

Chicken wire around a newly planted tree. (The chicken wire is 4 feet tall.)

Stakes or t-posts

You can do the same kind of fence on a smaller scale with other herbs & plants. You may want to have the chicken wire as a roof for the smaller plants.

Soli Deo Gloria!
—Julia

From the book:
The Holistic Homestead
© Copyright 2017 Julia Hubler
—ReformStead.com

210

Vegetables, Fruits & Herbs to Grow for Your Chickens

Fruit--Perennials	Vegetables /Fruit	Herbs	Greens	Grains/Seeds
Mulberries	Beets	Basil	Alfalfa	Sunflowers
Figs	Squash	Burdock	Lettuce	Amaranth
Apricots	Cabbage	Dill	Egyptian Spinach	Corn
Elderberries	Peas	Garlic	Moringa	Buckwheat
Blackberries	Green Beans	Lavender	Comfrey	Millet
Apples	Radishes	Marigold	Stinging Nettle	Sorghum
Pomegranates	Tomatoes	Marjoram	Kale	Cowpeas
Plums	Potatoes	Mint	Clover	
Peaches	Turnips	Oregano	Dandelion	
Pears	Cucumbers	Parsley	Yellow Mustard	
Wolf berries	Carrots	Rose Petals	Turnip Greens	
Dates	Melons	Rosemary	Radish Tops	
	Watermelon	Sage	Yellow Dock	
		Thyme	Purslane	
		Wormwood		

The Garden & Your Homestead

The garden is often the starting point of a homestead.

You can grow carbon (straw, dead plants, etc.) to mulch your garden and/or for the compost.

After harvest, dead plants can be chopped up and fed to your goats or laid on the soil as mulch. (Chop them really small if you're mulching bacterial soil.) You can also use them as carbon to make compost.

The garden gives food to beneficial insects and honey bees.

The garden provides your family with high quality produce.

The garden is a place to teach yourself and then your kids (or younger siblings) diligence & hard work.

Vegetables can be grown and fed to your animals. Greens, grains, squash (winter & summer), beets, carrots, etc. are great to feed to your cows, goats, sheep, pigs, chickens, other fowl & rabbits.

The garden may provide a place where you can put your chickens to work. They can eat bugs and clean up. Goats can clean up your after-harvest mess.

Soli Deo Gloria! —Julia

From the book:
R.S. The Holistic Homestead --Julia Hubler
--ReformStead.com
© Copyright 2017 Julia Hubler

RAIN & Greywater Ideas

For the Homestead

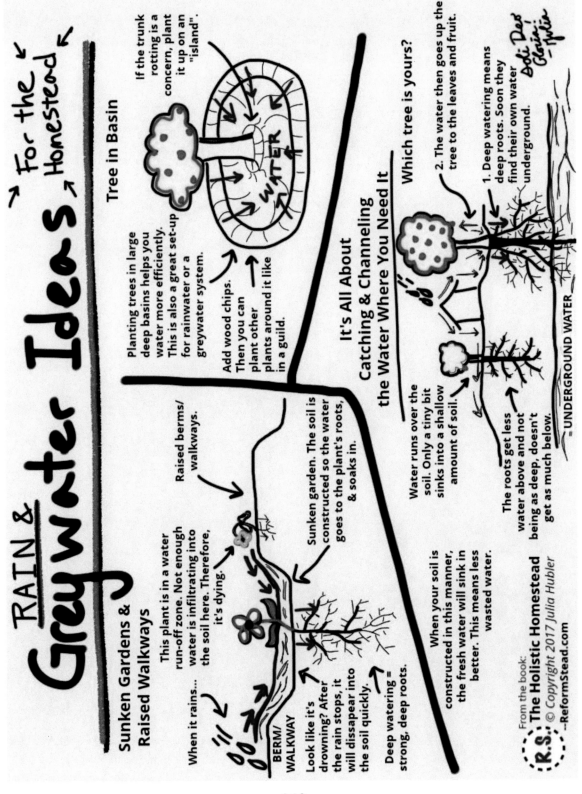

Sunken Gardens & Raised Walkways

This plant is in a water run-off zone. Not enough water is infiltrating into the soil here. Therefore, it's dying.

Raised berms/ walkways.

When it rains...

Look like it's drowning? After the rain stops, it will dissapear into the soil quickly.

Deep watering = strong, deep roots.

BERM/ WALKWAY

Sunken garden. The soil is constructed so the water goes to the plant's roots, & soaks in.

When your soil is constructed in this manner, the fresh water will sink in better. This means less wasted water.

Tree in Basin

If the trunk rotting is a concern, plant it up on an "island".

Planting trees in large deep basins helps you water more efficiently. This is also a great set-up for rainwater or a greywater system.

Add wood chips. Then you can plant other plants around it like in a guild.

WATER

It's All About Catching & Channeling the Water Where You Need It

Which tree is yours?

2. The water then goes up the tree to the leaves and fruit.

1. Deep watering means deep roots. Soon they find their own water underground.

Water runs over the soil. Only a tiny bit sinks into a shallow amount of soil.

The roots get less water above and not being as deep, doesn't get as much below.

~ = UNDERGROUND WATER

From the book:
R.S. The Holistic Homestead
© Copyright 2017 Julia Hubler
--ReformStead.com

Soli Deo Gloria! ~Julia

Greywater {cheap outdoor} SINK

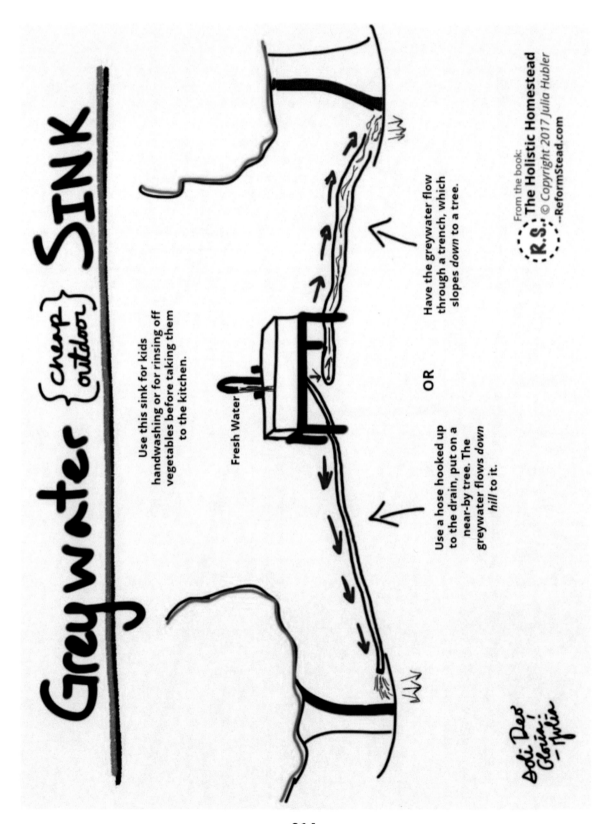

Use this sink for kids handwashing or for rinsing off vegetables before taking them to the kitchen.

Fresh Water

Have the greywater flow through a trench, which slopes *down* to a tree.

OR

Use a hose hooked up to the drain, put on a near-by tree. The greywater flows *down* hill to it.

From the book:
R.S. **The Holistic Homestead**
© Copyright 2017 Julia Hubler
--ReformStead.com

Soli Deo Gloria!
--Julia

Rainwater + Greywater & Your Homestead

Rainwater & Greywater are an amazing asset to the homestead.

Use rain & greywater to water fruit trees--or guilds.

Your shade & fruit trees benefit from the water-filtration-friendly soil construction and the extra water.

The fruit harvest from the trees is a great bonus!

Soil & land designed to receive rainwater means you'll use less fresh water. This saves money and water.

A homestead optimized for rain & greywater is greener and more productive.

Greywater is now a resource instead of liability.

When you harvest rain or greywater, more water is going into the soil--where it's suposed to be--which is good for the water table.

From the book:
The Holistic Homestead
© Copyright 2017 Julia Hubler
--ReformStead.com

R.S.

Soli Deo Gloria! —Julia

How To Find → CHICKEN Food on the Homestead

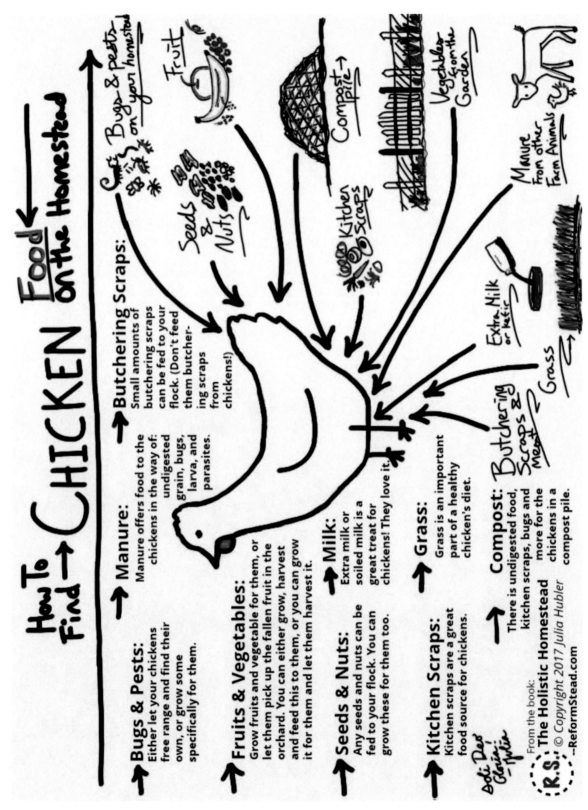

Bugs & Pests:
Either let your chickens free range and find their own, or grow some specifically for them.

Fruits & Vegetables:
Grow fruits and vegetable for them, or let them pick up the fallen fruit in the orchard. You can either grow, harvest and feed this to them, or you can grow it for them and let them harvest it.

Seeds & Nuts:
Any seeds and nuts can be fed to your flock. You can grow these for them too.

Kitchen Scraps:
Kitchen scraps are a great food source for chickens.

→ Manure:
Manure offers food to the chickens in the way of: undigested grain, bugs, larva, and parasites.

→ Butchering Scraps:
Small amounts of butchering scraps can be fed to your flock. (Don't feed them butchering scraps from chickens!)

→ Milk:
Extra milk or soiled milk is a great treat for chickens! They love it.

→ Grass:
Grass is an important part of a healthy chicken's diet.

Compost:
There is undigested food, kitchen scraps, bugs and more for the chickens in a compost pile.

Bugs & Pests on your homestead

Fruit

Seeds & Nuts

Compost Pile

Kitchen Scraps

Vegetables from the Garden

Manure from other Farm Animals

Extra Milk or kefir

Grass

Butchering Scraps & Meat

Soli Deo Gloria! —Julia

From the book:
The Holistic Homestead
© Copyright 2017 Julia Hubler
--ReformStead.com

R.S.

Holistic Chickens
Homestead

Chickens are often the first animals on a homestead.

Chickens add nitrogen to the compost, pasture, orchard and garden. (Wherever they go!)

They eat extra and overripe produce from the garden and orchard.

Chickens are a great start for the homestead. They work even better in unison with other fowls: guineas, geese and ducks.

Chickens provide your family with fresh eggs and/or meat.

They eat kitchen "wastes" such as food scraps, leftovers, milk, broth, etc.

Chickens can WORK on your homestead. They can tear down a compost pile, spread a pile of mulch, eat bugs, clean fallen fruit off the orchard floor, etc.

Chickens eat bugs, parasites, fly larva, scorpions, and more. They'll keep these away from your house, pastures, garden, and compost pile.

From the book:
R.S. The Holistic Homestead
© Copyright 2017 Julia Hubler
--ReformStead.com

Soli Deo Gloria! —Julia

Fowl on the Homestead

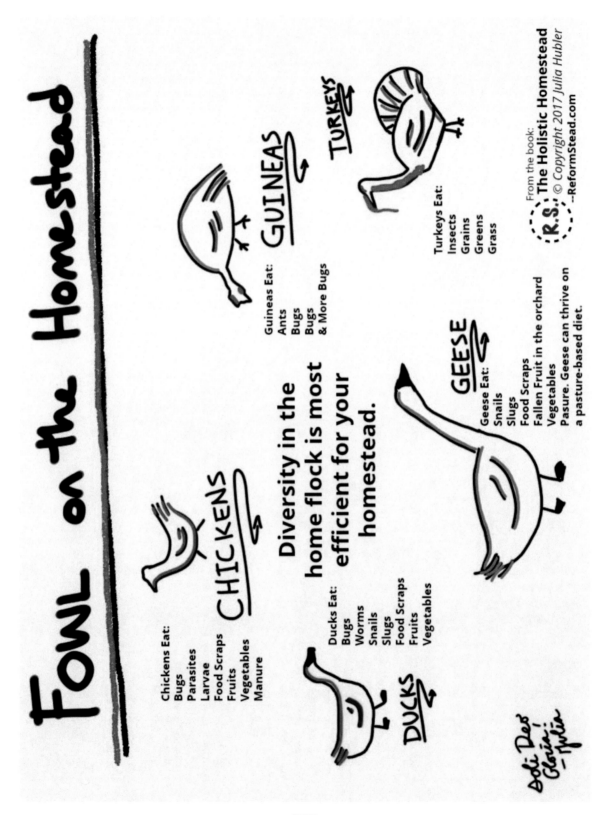

CHICKENS

Chickens Eat:
Bugs
Parasites
Larvae
Food Scraps
Fruits
Vegetables
Manure

DUCKS

Ducks Eat:
Bugs
Worms
Snails
Slugs
Food Scraps
Fruits
Vegetables

Diversity in the home flock is most efficient for your homestead.

GUINEAS

Guineas Eat:
Ants
Bugs
Bugs
& More Bugs

TURKEYS

Turkeys Eat:
Insects
Grains
Greens
Grass

GEESE

Geese Eat:
Snails
Slugs
Food Scraps
Fallen Fruit in the orchard
Vegetables
Pasure. Geese can thrive on a pasture-based diet.

From the book:
R.S. The Holistic Homestead
© Copyright 2017 Julia Hubler
--ReformStead.com

Soli Deo Gloria!
—Julia

Cows vs. Goats

Which is best for your homestead?

Milk Cow

Goats

- Cows are larger.
- Size may be a concern with your kids.
- They give more milk.

vs. They eat more.

- There's more manure.
- Most Americans are used to the taste of cow's milk.
- They're generally known as being sweet natured.
- They cost more to buy/own.
- They give lots of...

→ Cream!

Milk Goat

- Goats are smaller.
- They eat less.
- There's less manure.
- They give less milk.
- Some people don't like the taste of their milk.

Soli Deo Gloria! —Julia Hubler

COMPARE --> Just remember a combination-- diversity--is the best thing for your homestead.

- Goats have a repuation of being stubborn at times.
- No cream. Their milk doesn't separate.
- They cost less to buy & keep.

From the book:
The Holistic Homestead
R.S.: © Copyright 2017 Julia Hubler
--ReformStead.com

219

How Goats & Cows Relate to You
→ Homestead ←

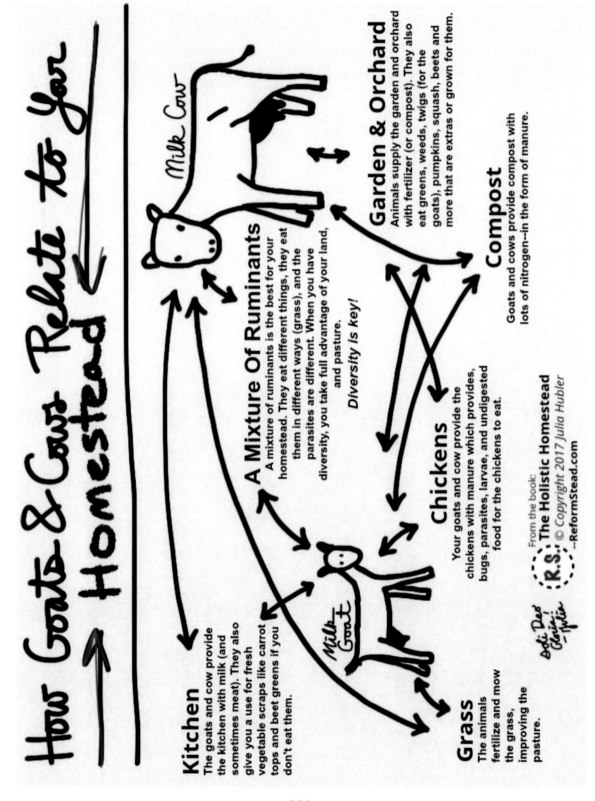

Milk Cow

Milk Goat

A Mixture Of Ruminants
A mixture of ruminants is the best for your homestead. They eat different things, they eat them in different ways (grass), and the parasites are different. When you have diversity, you take full advantage of your land, and pasture.

Diversity is key!

Kitchen
The goats and cow provide the kitchen with milk (and sometimes meat). They also give you a use for fresh vegetable scraps like carrot tops and beet greens if you don't eat them.

Grass
The animals fertilize and mow the grass, improving the pasture.

Chickens
Your goats and cow provide the chickens with manure which provides, bugs, parasites, larvae, and undigested food for the chickens to eat.

Garden & Orchard
Animals supply the garden and orchard with fertilizer (or compost). They also eat greens, weeds, twigs (for the goats), pumpkins, squash, beets and more that are extras or grown for them.

Compost
Goats and cows provide compost with lots of nitrogen--in the form of manure.

From the book:
The Holistic Homestead
© Copyright 2017 Julia Hubler
--ReformStead.com

Soli Deo Gloria!
--Julia

The Old-Fashioned Family Milk Cow
→ vs. ←
The Modern Commercial Dairy Cow

Soli Deo Gloria! —Julia

Cost:

Modern Cow
Lower up-front cost.

Old-Fashioned Cow
Much more expensive to start. View them as an investment.

Rumen:

Modern Cow
The majority of dairy cows are raised on milk (formula, most of the time), for only 4-6 weeks. Not long enough for the rumen to fully develop.

Old-Fashioned Cow
A good breeder will leave the calf on his dam for 4-6 months. This is required for proper rumen development.

There's more than just "buying a cow." Look into the genetics of the cow first. You may decide to get a cow from a dairy, but know what you're getting into.

Size:

Modern Cow
She can tip the scale at 1,500 pounds.

Old-Fashioned Cow
On average (although it depends on mini, mid-mini, small standard) she'll weigh 500-800 pounds.

Bred To Eat:

Modern Cow
She was bred to need lots of high concentrates (grains).

Old-Fashioned Cow
An old-fashioned cow has grazing genetics, meaning she'll thrive on a (mostly) grass diet.

Milk Quantity:

Modern Cow
Roughly 6-10 gallons a day

Old-Fashioned Cow
About 2-3 gallons a day

Life Expectancy:

Modern Cow
1.5-3 lactations is average in commercial dairies. It'll be longer on a healthy homestead, but still not as long as it should.

Old-Fashioned Cow
10-20 years

R.S. From the book:
The Holistic Homestead
© Copyright 2017 Julia Hubler
--ReformStead.com

Natural Remedies

For The FARMYARD

Just a few things to always have on hand!

Garlic

Garlic is:
Antibacterial
Antiviral
Worm preventer & treatment
An egg laying stimulant for chickens

Essential oils

Essential oils applied topically--diluted in a salve--to the udder can help fight mastitis. Peppermint, lavender and tea tree are good for both preventing and fighting masitits.

Vitamin C

Vitamin C is good for immunity and overall health. It's great to feed to any sick animal.

Molasses

Molasses is good for the rumen's health. It's also loaded with many other vitamins and minerals that are good for ruminant's health.

Coconut oil

Coconut oil is great for infections. This includes eye infections, mastitis and more.

Apple Cider Vinegar

ACV has:
Probiotics
Minerals & lots of potassium

ACV:
Is a great energy booster
It improves digestion
Supports the immune system
Is good for aches and sprains
Increases calcium and mineral absorption
Helps with respiratory health in chickens

kefir & yogurt

Both kefir and yogurt contain many good probiotics. These support the immune system and are great for the rumen.

Soli Deo Gloria!
—Julia

From the book:
The Holistic Homestead
© Copyright 2017 Julia Hubler
--ReformStead.com

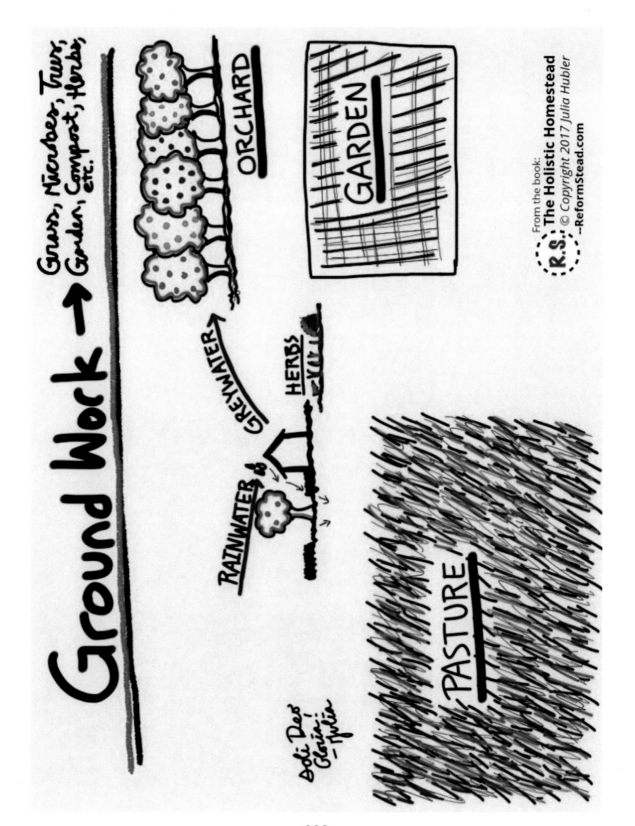

Ground Work

→ Grass, Microbes, Trees, Garden, Compost, Herbs, etc.

ORCHARD

GARDEN

GREYWATER

HERBS

RAINWATER

PASTURE

Soli Deo Gloria! —Julia

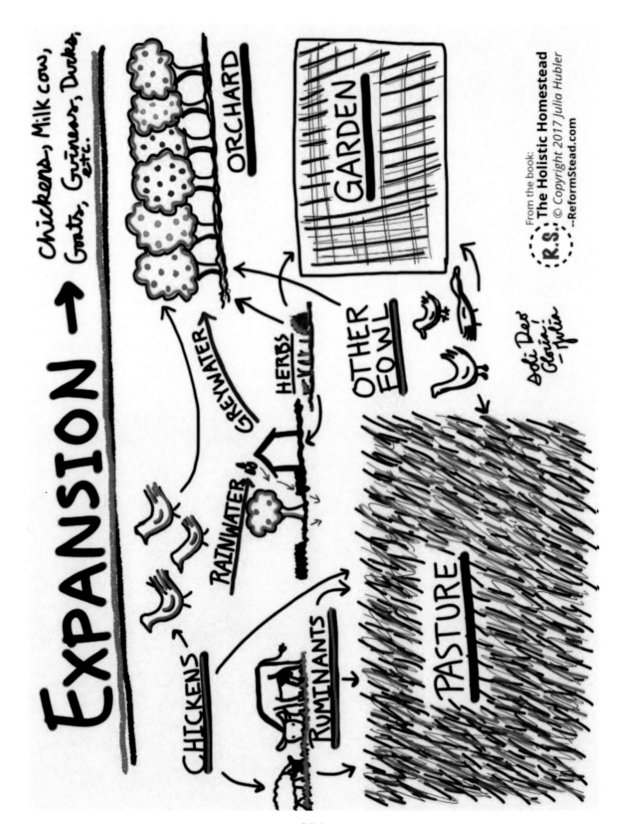

EXPANSION

Chickens, Milk cow, Goats, Guineas, Ducks, etc.

ORCHARD

GARDEN

GREYWATER

HERBS

OTHER FOWL

RAINWATER

CHICKENS

RUMINANTS

PASTURE

Soli Deo Gloria! —Julia

From the book:
R.S. The Holistic Homestead
© Copyright 2017 Julia Hubler
~ReformStead.com

Our Milk ROTATION SYSTEM

Fridge Shelf on the

Straight On View:

Reach to the back for the oldest milk.

← Newest

Even if this won't work in your fridge, think of how you could come up with something similar that will work for you.

Overhead View: Back of fridge

OLDEST →

If needed, turn the corner. ← jars of milk

OLDER →

← Newest

Keep the jars moving along the outer walls of the fridge. Put a few other food items in the middle.

From the book: The Holistic Homestead
R.S. © Copyright 2017 Julia Hubler --ReformStead.com

in the Fridge Door

Straight On View:

Bottom shelf in fridge door

NEWEST → → → OLDEST

Push the newer milk across as you use up the oldest.

Overhead View:

Bottom fridge door shelf

NEWEST → → → OLDEST

* Be careful not to weigh down the door too much! This would be great if you had a small amount of milk. Otherwise store milk on the main shelf.

Soli Deo Gloria! —Julia

Index

---> About <---

Hi! I'm Julia. First and foremost, I am a Christian. I desire to love and serve Jesus Christ the King in every area of my life. By His sovereignty, I live with my parents and five younger siblings in the *hot dry* desert of Phoenix, Arizona. We live on 2.5 acres, with summer highs often over 120 and zero percent humidity.

Every morning I wake up my siblings and we head out for chores. I give them jobs and keep them busy with gardening, milking and more for an hour every morning. If I can't find them a chore, they get off early, but I think they'd all tell you—*that's a rare day.*

I blog about my homesteading adventure at ReformStead.com—everything homesteading for the glory of God!

When I'm not milking goats, mulching fruit trees, or cooking dinner, you'll probably find me reading a book, listening to a sermon while sewing a jean skirt, playing a hymn or Vivaldi on my violin, taking photos and writing for my blog, or enjoying God's beautiful creation! *(For the last six months, I have been frantically writing a homesteading book. *smiley face*)*

That's about it. You'll find me raising guineas, making dinner, milking goats, and writing about it all, out on our piece of Arizona desert.

Soli Deo Gloria! *(Glory Be to God Alone!)*

-Julia